THE SMALL BUSINESS FINANCIAL PLANNER

THE SMALL BUSINESS FINANCIAL PLANNER

GREGORY R. GLAU

WILEY

John Wiley & Sons, Inc.

New York · Chichester · Brisbane · Toronto · Singapore

Publisher: Stephen Kippur
Editor: Katherine Schowalter
Managing Editor: Corinne McCormick
Editing, Design, and Production: G&H SOHO, Ltd.

This publication is designed to provide accurate and authoritative
information in regard to the subject matter covered. It is sold with the
understanding that the publisher is not engaged in rendering legal, accounting,
or other professional service. If legal advice or other expert assistance is
required, the services of a competent professional person should be sought.
*From a declaration of principles jointly adopted by a committee of the
American Bar Association and a committee of publishers.*

Library of Congress Cataloging-in-Publication Data

Glau, Gregory R.
  The small business financial planner.

  Bibliography: p.
  1. Small business—Finance. I. Title.
HG4027.7.G57 1989   658.1'592   88-20759
ISBN 0-471-63106-X

Printed in the United States of America

89 90 10 9 8 7 6 5 4 3 2 1

For Phyllis and Byron
—I love you

Contents

Contents

Introduction

For some reason, once your start your own company, you're automatically expected to understand all the financial information about your business. Much of it is pretty easy: You have to know what your costs are, how to add a percentage markup, the difference between gross and net profit, which expenses are direct costs and which belong in the overhead column, and so on.

But most small-business owners didn't go to business school, so when a term such as *current ratio, acid test,* or *inventory turnover* comes up, they're not sure exactly what it means or how to calculate the figure, much less what it might say about their company. When the business owner applies for a loan and the banker asks about the firm's earnings before interests and taxes or wonders how much cash flow the company has in relation to the current portion of its long-term debt, it can get confusing.

Financial analysis is also one thing many business owners often do by the seat of their pants. If enough cash seems to be coming in, why worry about it? If the company usually pays its bills on time, there can't be a problem with its collections and costs, can there? If cash seems a little tight now and then and the business has to borrow money, but the profit line on the income statement looks good, there's nothing to worry about, is there?

Well, *maybe there is.* The problem is that the successful business owner must somehow be able to look into the future and have a good idea of how the company will be doing in six months or a year. One of the best ways to forecast your own business future, and to prevent problems before they get started, is to keep a running record of how you've done in the past. The past does mirror the future, and if you know when and why your company had problems or good financial times, you'll be better able to avoid the difficulties and reproduce the good times—and their profit. Isn't that the whole idea?

Your business is probably seasonal, at least to some degree: You sell more at certain times of the year than others. Do you know how much more? Do you know exactly what those good times contribute to the overall success of your company? Wouldn't you find this out by tracking sales and costs and gross profit and net profit over time? Once you did that—and especially if you graphed the data—you would be able to see exactly when your sales were good and when they were not. You could tell when your costs increased (which means you needed more cash during those periods) and when your cash inflow was enough to pay everything. You would know when your business was making a profit and what times of the year it was running in the red.

Unless you follow the information, there's no way to tell when there are problems. And if you don't know when those difficult times occur, there's no way to correct them. On the good side, if you don't know during which periods your business does well, how can you capitalize on that trend?

That's the secret to preventing financial problems: to track specific financial data that's useful to you, so you know what's happening *before* you have a problem. If every month you make the right comparisons and watch for variations from the norm, you're right on top of things and can fix them before you develop a major difficulty. You *see* your future when something in your financial picture starts to deviate from what's been normal for it—and that's what the worksheets and graphs in this book will help you with.

What This Book Covers

How is your profit? Not just your net profit, but your gross profit? That's the true measure of how well you're handling your direct costs and the factor that determines whether you can pay your overhead. Does your gross profit accurately reflect the markup you put on what you sell? Chapter 1 focuses on profit, so you'll know exactly where yours comes from and how to increase it.

Are there times of the year when you seem to have enough sales but not enough cash? This situation is known as a *liquidity squeeze* and simply means your business doesn't have enough of its assets in the form of cash at the right time. How to know when those times are and how much cash your company requires is detailed in Chapter 2.

You know what *cash flow* means . . . don't you? The definition may not be exactly what you think it is, because cash flow, like net profit, is affected by debt. Chapter 3 outlines how to calculate your cash flow and how it relates to your debt. It also tells you exactly how much more debt your company might be able to handle.

Chapter 4 covers business ratios—those figures your banker uses all the time. Ratios are a key to how well you're doing, and once you know what information to follow and how to examine it, you'll find they really can forecast your business future. Ratios make it easy to compare your company with others too, so you can see how you're doing in relation to your peers.

Costs are always a problem for any company, especially *direct* costs—the second-largest figure on your income statement. The wise business owner understands all cost details and knows how to plan to decrease costs for the company. Chapter 5 focuses on costs, how you can pinpoint yours, and how to lower them.

Unless you have a lot of money, sooner or later you'll have to borrow some cash for your business. Borrowing is also known as *leverage,* and if used properly, it can increase profits. But there are two parts to the leverage equation, and Chapter 6 tells you what to watch for on both sides of the scale.

Chapter 7 focuses on how you can prevent problems in the two vital areas where cash seems to get stuck in many businesses: inventory and accounts receivable. Knowing how to speed up the movement of cash through both of these areas can really have an impact on your cash flow and profit.

When you started or purchased your business, you probably created a worksheet that forecasted your sales and determined the costs and overhead required to break even. This analysis is a bit of work, but it tells you *exactly* the figures you must record just to break even. It also lets you simulate what might happen to your break-even level under different sets of circumstances. Chapter 8 demonstrates how to do a break-even analysis for your business and also shows how you can—easily—create those complex-looking break-even graphs.

Every business owner wants to to have the best machinery, vehicles, and equipment but can justify their purchase only if they will pay for themselves. Chapter 9 outlines how you can tell if a fixed asset will increase your company's productivity.

What you sell and who you sell to obviously determine whether your company is successful. Sadly, some business owners don't give sales a lot of consideration. They're in, say, the appliance business, so that's what they sell: appliances. They never determine which areas of their company produce a profit for the business and which are loss-leaders. Chapter 10 shows you how to discover this information and what it means in real dollars.

Chapter 11 gives you a new idea of the way budgets are created, one that lets you forecast your company's future accuracy. By combining your expected budget with actual cost items as they're recorded, you can get a much better picture of your financial future, and your banker will be more likely to approve the loan you need.

How to Use This Book

Success in a small business is an ongoing process that should begin when the firm is started. If your company's been around for a time, start tracking your financial data right now. If it's not too difficult to go through your records and get some past history, do so. The idea is to build a base of financial information that focuses on your own company and that you can use for specific types of analysis.

You'll find two kinds of figures in this book: worksheets and graphs. You can create a number of worksheets that focus on specific financial information. The worksheets are partly filled in to give you a sense of what they look like as they're being used. The blank spots on the grids are there to give you an idea of how to design and customize the worksheets for your own company.

Once information starts to accumulate, it's often hard to read through all the numbers and understand what they mean, so I suggest that you graph them. A graph will give you a moving picture of your own facts and figures. Many of the worksheets are directly linked to graphs to help you see the connection between the two.

Something you should do on a continual basis is to compare your business's current figures with its own historical average and with the industry average. One way to do this is to start with a graph that plots just the averages. Mark them across the chart for several years (they'll be straight, flat lines) and then plot your monthly information on the picture.

Each chapter focuses on a fictional company and uses examples with real-world numbers. You can see how the worksheets are filled in and can work your way through financial data along with the owners of these businesses. You'll learn how to use the charts and worksheets as a prevention tool that will pinpoint problems in your own company before they get serious.

Following the text is a glossary to help you fully understand the terms used.

Data on the industry you're in is available from industry magazines or from the *Annual Statement Studies*. This book (from Robert Morris Associates, P.O. Box 8500, S-1140, Philadelphia, PA 19178) lists ratio and other percentage figures collected from small-business financial statements given to banks across the country. Businesses are grouped by industry and by the size of their sales volume. The *Annual Statement Studies* is available in most libraries.

Every business is different, and by comparing yours with the norm, you'll find where your own strengths and weaknesses lie. That's the secret of business success: to eliminate your weaknesses and to capitalize on your strengths. This book will show you how.

1

The Business of
Your Numbers

If you're like most business owners, when you receive the income statement for your company, your eyes immediately fall to the bottom line, the figure that shows whether you made a profit or loss for the period detailed on the statement.

Looking at your profit (or lack of it) is the logical place to start any examination of your business's financial information. Where do your profits come from? Why did your business record the numbers it did? How do all your costs affect that bottom line? What is your company's earning power, and how do you calculate it? The secret is to know which numbers are important to your business and which are not. That's the only hard part about working with a company's financial information—knowing which questions to ask.

Why do you need to record a profit? Well, of course, that's the whole idea of being in business, but more than that, consider a company that doesn't make money, a business that instead loses it. What happens? Obviously, sooner or later, the business will run out of cash and will have to close its doors. So there's nothing complicated about why a company needs to record a profit: It's the only way it can survive. Profit is a hedge to *prevent* future financial problems. Sure, you might break even for a time, by recording sales figures that exactly equal your cost totals, but unless you make a profit that can work against those times when you do lose money (and every company has them), you'll end up closing your doors.

The first thing to do is to compare the profit you record to your own historical data. Is your company making a better or worse profit than it has in the past? If there is some change, you'll want to find out why. The second is to compare your profit to that of other companies in your industry. Are you doing a better or worse job than your peers at using the assets you have available, in terms of creating profits? That's important to know, because your banker will make the same comparisons and will judge whether your company deserves a loan on that basis.

If you find any deviation in your current numbers from either your historical average or how others in your industry are doing, it's a warning sign that something isn't quite right.

This isn't to say that there's something wrong if you start to record higher profits than you have in the past. On the contrary, that's what every business owner works for. A deviation in either direction just tells you that your company, for some reason, has moved away from what's been normal for it. Perhaps you've lowered costs—that's good. Possibly your overhead has increased—that's not so good. But unless you have a systematic way to track your financial data and then make logical comparisons to your own past information and/or industry figures, you'll never know when your current numbers take a wrong turn. Unless you know when this happens, how can you do anything to correct it? If the numbers make a change for the better, unless you know about it (and why they're different), you won't be able to capitalize on the shift as effectively as possible.

Case Study: Second Chance Clothing

Second Chance Clothing is both a typical and not-so-typical business. Your company is probably similar in that it's got its own unusual characteristics, departments, sales techniques, and so on. Fran, the owner of Second Chance Clothing, takes in clothing on consignment and pays people only when the items are sold. When a customer brings something into the store, it must be clean and in near-new condition. The business isn't like a thrift shop but instead a place where dresses, skirts, pants, shirts, coats, and such are recycled.

When someone's clothing sells, the customer receives, on average, 60% of its selling price, and Second Chance Clothing makes 40%. It's an interesting idea, as this part of the business has no direct costs. Since everything in this department is on consignment, the company makes no purchases, so, in essence, it has no inventory investment.

Is this an idea you might use in your own company? The idea

of clothing on consignment might sound unusual, but how about the equipment your business sells? Many appliance manufacturers (including heating firms, companies that produce washing machines and dryers, room air-conditioning units, and so on) offer consignment or floor plans, putting merchandise in a warehouse and showroom at little or no cost to the dealer. The dealer doesn't pay for it until he or she sells it. Some manufacturers even offer programs that let you change your inventory mix from summer to winter, so you always have the right merchandise in stock for the time of the year. Even if you have to pay a small interest charge, that old truism that says you'll sell what you have on hand is so often true that the cost of consignment items is usually insignificant in relation to the extra sales you'll record.

From an overhead standpoint, Second Chance's cost for displaying the merchandise is the same no matter who the clothing belongs to. What this approach does is let the business work with other people's money, as the only investment the business needs is for racks and other display items.

Fran also purchases some of the used clothing people bring in, which becomes inventory for the business. Lately, Second Chance Clothing has also started buying new clothing items.

Fran, therefore, has three distinct departments that the company sells from: consignment items, used clothing she purchased, and new clothing.

This business, then, is like many others in that it has an inventory investment that it sells at retail—but with a kicker: The consignment items have an overhead expense but no direct cost. Even though Fran's business is different from your own, you'll be able to apply many of the same profit-control techniques that she uses to your own company.

Keeping Track of Profits

Once your eyes leave the last line of your income statement and start to read the rest of it, you'll see two profit areas listed. One is what you saw at the bottom—your *net profit*—and the other is your *gross profit* (also called your gross margin). That's the profit your business recorded before any operating expenses (also called overhead) were removed.

Normally, your gross profit in percentage terms should equal your markup. If you put a 33% markup on the products you sell, you should record a gross profit of 33%. That's the way things should work, but in most cases, they don't—your gross margin is often lower than your markup. The difference is the amount, in dollars, of things that were ruined, lost, stolen, not charged to the right work order, and so on.

Figure 1-1 is a worksheet used by Second Chance Clothing to keep track of its gross and net profit performance on a quarterly basis. It gives Fran a feel for the company's performance in relation to its own average as well as that of other clothing stores. That data is extracted from the *Annual Statement Studies.* This book, produced for the banking industry, is a yearly detailed accounting of financial statements provided by member banks. The business categories are coded, which means you can look up information for businesses in the same line as your own. Bankers, as you might expect, use the data in this annual survey to help them decide how to handle loan applications.

For instance, if you're in the retail clothing business (say, women's ready-to-wear) and your business applies for a loan, your banker will look up information about other companies in the same line of work that are doing about the same sales volume you are. The banker can then see how much, as a percentage of sales, the average business in your field pays its officers; the average of its direct costs in relation to sales; its usual overhead; and so on. If your figures are out of line—in either direction—the banker will wonder about your loan application. That's why it's so important to know not only your own figures but what others in your field are also recording.

Figure 1-1 shows that during the first quarter Second Chance Clothing recorded sales of $180,000, along with a gross profit of $57,000, which is 31.7% of sales. This information tells Fran what her average markup was during this time. Fran's cost for her inventory and its retail value should be the same: 31.7%. If the average markup for all of Fran's inventory was, say, 34%, then some clothing items were lost through theft or because they got ruined or weren't marked up correctly in the first place. If your business records a gross margin that is less than its average markup, you also can assume that things are being lost, stolen, ruined, priced improperly, or not charged to your customers.

It's impossible to record a gross profit higher than your average markup, since you can never sell inventory for more than its price.

```
!---------------------------------------------------------------!
!                 Profit (before taxes) worksheet              !
!                                                               !
!  First Quarter                                                !
!  -------------                                                !
!                      Sales    Gross profit   Net profit       !
!  amount ->          180,000      57,000         6,000         !
!  % of sales ->        100%       31.7%          3.3%          !
!                                                               !
!                                                               !
!      Gross profit:                   Variance:                !
!      Historical average  30.0%         1.7%                   !
!      Industry average    29.0%         2.7%                   !
!                                                               !
!      Net profit:                     Variance:                !
!      Historical average   3.0%          .3%                   !
!      Industry average     2.5%          .8%                   !
!                                                               !
!===============================================================!
!                                                               !
!  Second Quarter                                               !
!  --------------                                               !
!                      Sales    Gross profit   Net profit       !
!  amount ->          200,000      59,000         4,000         !
!  % of sales ->        100%       29.5%          2.0%          !
!                                                               !
!                                                               !
!      Gross profit:                   Variance:                !
!      Historical average  30.0%        - .5%                   !
!      Industry average    29.0%          .5%                   !
!                                                               !
!      Net profit:                     Variance:                !
!      Historical average   3.0%         -.5%                   !
!      Industry average     2.5%         -.5%                   !
!                                                               !
!===============================================================!
!                                                               !
!  Third Quarter                                                !
!  -------------                                                !
!                      Sales    Gross profit   Net profit       !
!  amount ->         [_____]     [_____]      [_____]        !
!  % of sales ->     [_____]     [_____]      [_____]        !
!                                                               !
!                                                               !
!      Gross profit:                   Variance:                !
!      Historical average [_____]        [_____]                !
!      Industry average   [_____]        [_____]                !
!                                                               !
!      Net profit:                     Variance:                !
!      Historical average [_____]        [_____]                !
!      Industry average   [_____]        [_____]                !
!                                                               !
!===============================================================!
```

Figure 1-1 Profit before taxes worksheet.

Second Chance Clothing's net profit during the first quarter was $6,000, or 3.3%. The lower part of each section of the worksheet lists the historical and industry averages, as well as any variances in the information. These details— the deviation from the norm— are important because any change signals that the way the company has been doing business is different. Changes are an indication that the business owner needs to look a bit more closely at the information to find out why there's a variance.

If it's a change for the better, you'd want to continue to do the same things (or more along the same line). If the change is for the worse, you'd want to take steps to turn the situation around.

In Figure 1-1, it's easy to see that for the first quarter the company recorded a gross and a net profit a bit higher than average, both from a historical standpoint and in comparison to other businesses in the industry. During the second quarter all the figures were slightly lower. The variances aren't great in either direction and probably indicate the normal ebb and flow of the business cycle. What a business needs to be concerned with is a trend, whether it's upward or downward. Usually, the easiest way to see the overall direction of a lot of numbers is to graph them. Fran plots the information from these worksheets in Figure 1-2.

Figure 1-2 shows the gross profit percentage for Second Chance Clothing over a two-year period. The line that varies, marked with small boxes, represents the company's gross profit percentage. The straight line that runs across at 30% and is marked with plus signs represents the company's historical average. The line that runs across at 29% and is marked with small diamonds is the average gross profit for the line of work Fran is in. As mentioned earlier, these figures can be extracted from the *Annual Statement Studies* or from industry trade publications.

This is the kind of picture that should disturb any business owner for several reasons. First, starting in the third quarter, the company's gross profit average was lower than both its historical average and the industry average. Second, while there are some minor ups and downs in the data, it appears to have a general downward slope. That tells Fran that the business's gross profit, on average, is declining.

Third, the company's own average along with that of the industry it operates in provide a range on the picture. These averages appear on Figure 1-2 as two straight lines. In most cases, if your data is where it should be—in line with your own and industry figures—it will plot within or very close to this range. If the numbers move away

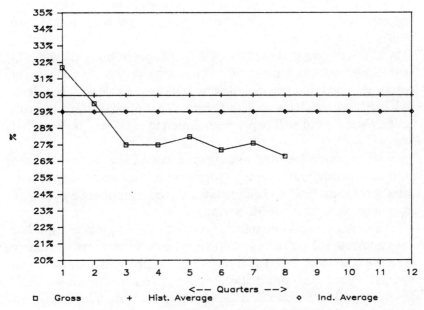

Figure 1-2 Gross profit percentage line graph.

from this area for some reason, the graph makes the shift easy to spot the moment it happens.

Finally, Fran took too long before taking some action, suggesting that her business isn't being managed well. She should have spotted the drop after the third quarter's data was recorded. At that time, Fran needed to discover why the gross margin was falling. Never wait this late in the game—after your gross profit had fallen and then remained lower than average for a year and a half—before doing something to reverse the trend.

Managing Direct and Indirect Costs

That's the first lesson to be learned from Second Chance Clothing: Information must be tracked on a regular basis, or it soon becomes too late to correct a problem. In this case, if Fran had been monitoring the data both on worksheets and as a graph, the problem with her gross profit would have been easy to spot. It would have been easier to fix early on, too. Now the company's been operating at a lower gross profit margin for some time, which means it has less money to do business with. That only aggravates the company's problems. The idea here is really twofold: First, to learn how to prevent a falling gross/net profit situation, and second, to know how to deal with it if it does occur.

How can you prevent your gross or net profit margin from falling? Gross profit is a function of your sales related to your direct costs—the costs that you can directly trace to your sales. If you don't sell anything, you have no direct costs. What determines your gross profit, then, is your selling price in relation to what you pay for what you sell.

If you can raise your selling prices and at the same time keep your costs steady, you'll increase your gross profit margin. If you keep sales at the same level and can somehow drop your direct costs, you'll also raise your gross profit margin.

The net profit you record is related to your gross margin less your indirect (often called overhead) costs. If you can somehow decrease your overhead, you'll raise your net profit. If your overhead rises, and your gross profit stays the same, your net profit will fall. Let's get back to Second Chance Clothing and take a look at its net profit.

What happened to net profit during this same period? Fran plots that in Figure 1–3, and the image isn't quite as disturbing. The actual data is shown as the line marked with small boxes. The company's historical average for net profit is marked with plus signs and runs across the graph at 3%. The industry average is marked with diamonds and runs across the picture at 2.5%.

For the first five quarters shown, Fran managed to keep net profit within its average range. During the period when gross profit fell drastically, the business somehow kept net profit at a higher (percentage) level. Only for the last three quarters has net profit fallen, and even at that, the last plot shows a definite rise, as it appears to be headed back toward its normal operating area.

What does all this mean? First, you know that Second Chance Clothing's gross profit is off, lower than its historical and industry average. Net profit has fallen, too, just as you'd expect, but not as dramatically. Why not? Since a small change in the gross margin has a huge impact on net profit, Fran concludes that the company's overhead has also been falling. Otherwise the profit line would have dropped at the same rate that the gross profit margin did.

The net and gross profit lines show Fran that the problem is

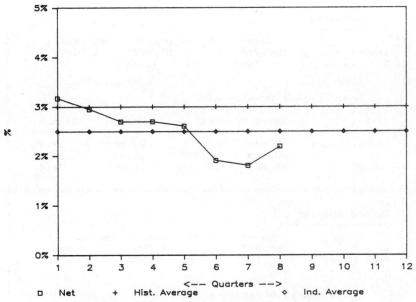

Figure 1–3 Net profit percentage line graph.

with the company's direct costs. They're higher than expected, so they're producing a smaller gross profit margin. Once Fran knows this, she can concentrate on the data that reflects those direct costs (and thus gross profit). Let's look at a more detailed worksheet to see where and why Second Chance Clothing's direct costs are higher than they have been.

Figure 1–4 breaks down the gross profit margin for each area of the business. The blank area on the bottom of this worksheet (like others in this book) is for you to use to help you track the information for your own company. Like most businesses with specific areas that fall into logical categories, Second Chance Clothing keeps separate track of each of its three departments: consignment items, new clothing, and used clothing.

The consignment clothing area, of course, had no direct costs, so its direct cost line is blank. For the first quarter, this department produced a gross profit of 37.3%, new clothing had a 30% gross margin average, and the used clothing department had a 24.4% average.

The second quarter's information shows that the consignment

```
.-----------------------------------------------------------.
!                                                           !
!                Gross profit worksheet                     !
!                                                           !
!  First Quarter                                            !
!  -------------                                            !
!                                                           !
!                    Sales     Gross profit   Net profit    !
!    amount ->       180,000      57,000         6,000       !
!    % of sales ->     100%        31.7%          3.3%       !
!                                                           !
!                                                           !
!      Gross profit breakdown:                              !
!                                                           !
!                    Sales     Cost       Gross    Margin    !
!                    --------------------------------------  !
!    Consignment    75,000   [_____]   28,000    37.3%      !
!    New            60,000   42,000     18,000    30.0%      !
!    Used           45,000   38,500     11,000    24.4%      !
!                                                           !
!===========================================================!
!                                                           !
!  Second Quarter                                           !
!  --------------                                           !
!                                                           !
!                    Sales     Gross profit   Net profit    !
!    amount ->       200,000      59,000         4,000       !
!    % of sales ->     100%        29.5%          2.0%       !
!                                                           !
!                                                           !
!      Gross profit breakdown:                              !
!                                                           !
!                    Sales     Cost       Gross    Margin    !
!    Consignment    80,000   [_____]   35,000    43.8%      !
!    New            65,000   54,000     11,000    16.9%      !
!    Used           55,000   42,000     13,000    23.6%      !
!===========================================================!
!                                                           !
!  Third Quarter                                            !
!  -------------                                            !
!                    Sales     Gross profit   Net profit    !
!    amount ->     [_____]     [_____]      [_____]      !
!    % of sales -> [_____]     [_____]      [_____]      !
!                                                           !
!                                                           !
!      Gross profit breakdown:                              !
!                                                           !
!                    Sales     Cost       Gross    Margin    !
!    Consignment [_____]   [_____]   [_____]   [_____]     !
!    New         [_____]   [_____]   [_____]   [_____]     !
!    Used        [_____]   [_____]   [_____]   [_____]     !
!                                                           !
!===========================================================!
```

Figure 1-4 Gross profit worksheet.

area recorded an average gross margin of 43.8%, new clothing was down sharply to 16.9%, and used clothing stayed about the same at 23.6%.

The biggest drop is in the new-clothing area. Its direct costs show that this department had problems during this quarter. While its sales were only slightly higher during the second quarter, its costs rose drastically. Why?

If Fran were to examine her company's records for this period, she might find several things that could cause such a jump in direct costs. (If you find a similar problem in your own business, these are the same places you'd want to examine.) One thing she should examine is a huge inventory purchase that she made late in the quarter, too late to add to sales volume for the period. If she makes such a purchase, then the cost ratio should fall during the following quarter and things should average out. If a large inventory purchase was recorded (it's easy to find out by looking at inventory records), Fran would want to wait one more quarter to see that the new-clothing department's average margin came up to where it usually is. If so, the company would know that whatever was purchased was adding to the business's sales total. If the average margin *didn't* rebound, then Fran would want to take a hard look at her inventory selection and pricing, because whatever the business bought, it wasn't selling.

On the negative side, Fran might learn that the poor margin was caused by too low of a markup for the items sold from this department. She might have priced her new clothing lower than she should have, perhaps because of more competition or because she didn't know what the true product costs were.

Thus two things can cause the sales-to-cost ratio to fall: acquiring too much inventory that doesn't sell and setting selling prices that don't reflect the true costs of the merchandise.

Finding Your Business's Problem Areas

As information starts to accumulate, it becomes easier to understand in the form of a graph. For Second Chance Clothing, it makes sense to plot the gross profit percentages of each of its three departments. The graph gives Fran something of a moving picture of her company's figures and allows her to see how each department performs over a period of time.

Figure 1–5 plots data for the gross profit margins for each of the three areas of Second Chance Clothing. The flat lines that run across the picture represent the averages for each data set.

The highest line is for the consignment clothing. Current information, for the fifteen months shown, is marked with small boxes. Gross profit for this area of the company has remained right around

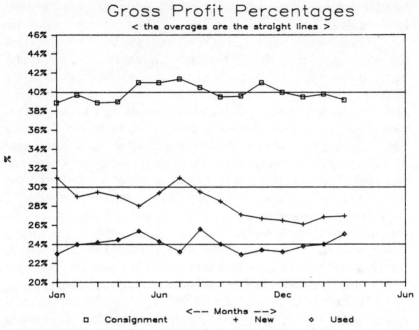

Figure 1–5 Gross profit percentages line graph.

its 40% average, which is just what you'd expect. This part of the company, with no investment, should make the highest gross profit.

Actually, there should be only minor variations in this data for Second Chance Clothing, as every customer works on the same percentage: The customer receives 60% of the selling price, and Fran's business gets 40%. However, some things are lost through theft or because they're ruined, and there is often some negotiation on price for these products, so a slight rise and fall of the line is natural.

The lowest line, which represents used clothing that the company purchased for resale, also stayed close to its average gross profit of 24% over this fifteen-month period. While that's a lower markup than many businesses like to use, perhaps it's necessary for Second Chance Clothing; maybe that's the best markup someone can get on used clothing.

If this profit comparison seems contradictory—since the consignment items average a 40% gross margin—consider that the consignment products represent no investment to the company. That means they can be allowed to remain in stock for a longer period than the used clothing. The consignment items can wait, so to speak, until someone who's willing to pay the asking price comes along.

Used clothing (like products in the new-clothing department) has to move, or the business won't make any money on its investment. Sometimes, a lower markup is the only way keep inventory turning.

As Fran suspected, there's a definite problem with the new-clothing department of the business. Its line, the center one marked with plus signs on Figure 1–5, bounced along close to its 30% average until July, then fell through the bottom and headed lower. The department's gross profit as a percentage of its sales is now down about 4% lower than its historical average. That means, as noted earlier, Fran's got a problem with her markup and/or the cost of the items in the new-clothing department. Since at this point overhead isn't removed from the figures, the only things that affect gross profit are the cost of what's sold and its selling price.

The solution for a falling gross profit margin is to know the exact cost of everything you handle before you mark it up for sale. In Fran's case, Second Chance Clothing should make sure (1) that the invoice price for each item is correct, (2) that the products cannot be purchased elsewhere at a lower cost, (3) that all direct costs, including freight, are added to the cost of the product before the item is marked up, and (4) that the business isn't losing inventory through theft, damage, and so on.

In your own business, perhaps employees are careless with parts and supplies; some of them might get ruined or forgotten about as they're carried around in your trucks. By the time you take a physical inventory and discover these lost products, they're too beat up to sell. Others get thrown away. Or your service technicians don't list every part they use when they're repairing something, so the customer doesn't get billed for everything that should have been charged to the job. Maybe some customers are walking out the door with part of your inventory hidden under their coats. Perhaps whoever does your ordering isn't handling it efficiently, so your transportation costs add much more than you realize to your inventory cost. If you sell by mail order, maybe you'd be better off using United Parcel Service exclusively and forgetting about the post office. If you deliver what you sell to your customers, perhaps there's a less expensive method of doing so—smaller vehicles, better planning in terms of routing, and so on.

In my own business, all of these problems come along at one time or another. For example, the employees who install new furnaces don't write down everything they use, so the job billing is incorrect. These people aren't dishonest; they're just forgetful. It's all too easy to unload a truck and throw out good parts with the trash. When the company schedules service calls, an effort must be made to route the service technicians so there's as little backtracking as possible. If you have people out driving around, how often do they cover the same miles, going the other direction? Perhaps better planning would eliminate some of those trips, as well as their gas and maintenance costs.

Check your vehicles—you'll be amazed at what you'll find, particularly if you have service trucks. Parts that were intended to be used for a specific job weren't needed, but they're left in the truck instead of being returned to stock. In-warranty parts, which must be sent back to the manufacturer for credit, haven't been brought in, either; they're still knocking around inside the truck. That means the company paid for the replacement part and never got credit for the defective one—a double cost.

If you have a problem with your direct inventory costs, and your markup hasn't dropped for a special sale or some other reason, then the difficulty probably lies with the way you handle what you carry in stock. It gets lost, isn't charged to the job, or gets ruined.

The other thing that affects your gross profit ratio is, of course, your total sales. If you keep adding to your inventory or increasing your other direct costs but sales stagnate, your gross profit will decrease. That's easy to spot—you'll know when your sales drop.

You can't tell from the data in Figure 1–5 whether Second Chance Clothing paid too much for what it had in its new-clothing department, used an incorrect markup, discounted things it shouldn't have, or had some items stolen or ruined. You can tell, however, that one of these things accounts for the company's problems with its gross profit. Once you know where to look for problems, you can find and fix them.

How to Figure Out Your Earning Power

In addition to examining how your business is producing gross and net profit, you should take a look at another set of figures that measures how effective you are as a manager. It calculates your business's *earning power* and measures how effectively you use available assets without any regard to the sources of those assets. Good management of assets is a key to the prevention of financial problems:

If you can keep what assets you have working as they should, you'll be getting awfully close to a problem-free company.

The calculation of the earning power ratio will tell you exactly how effectively you're managing your assets. Once you have this figure, you can compare it to your own past performance as well as to that of others in your industry.

To calculate your business's earning power, you must consider two things: your operating margin and the turnover of your operation assets. Your earning power is equal to your operating margin multiplied by the turnover rate of the operating assets you employ.

Your *operating margin* is the percentage you get when you divide your net profit by your sales volume. Your operating margin differs from net profit if you have any extraordinary items in the total during the period under study. For example, if your company sold a building, that's not *operating* revenue, as it wasn't produced through the normal course of business operations. For most small companies, the net profit before taxes equals the operating income. Before you calculate the net profits before taxes ratio, however, you should make sure that if there are some unique transactions during the period, you remove their amounts.

A company with annual sales of $500,000 and a net profit margin of $20,000 for that same period would have an operating margin of $20,000/$500,000, or 4.0%. Put another way—one the business owner doesn't always consider—this means that four cents of each dollar of sales turn into profit. If you sell something for one dollar, you'll have only four cents left over after your direct costs and overhead are paid.

The operating income/sales ratio is listed in the *Annual Statement Studies* as Profit Before Taxes but without any extraordinary items removed. However, you can compare it to your own figures to get at least an idea of what other companies like yours record.

The second part of your earning power ratio is determined by the turnover of your operating assets—those assets you use to create sales. Normally, a small business uses all of its assets in its pursuit of sales, but this is not always the case. You might, for example, own some land that you plan to build a building on. The investment you'd have to make—including both the down payment and any monthly payments—isn't doing a thing to help your sales volume, so it's not considered to be an operating asset. This is another reason to track your investments on a monthly basis: Your company may be making payments on things that are assets, but they're not operating assets and therefore should be removed from the figures before you calculate your earning power.

Perhaps you have some machinery that your company used at one time but doesn't any longer. That means it's not an operating asset, as it's not helping to produce sales. Possibly you rent out part of a building you own to other businesses. That share of your income is not operating income, and the proportion of the building (and its payment) that's being rented out isn't an operating asset (unless your primary business is renting space). To summarize, anything that you use to make sales is considered to be an operating asset; anything that doesn't help, isn't.

The following formula calculates the amount of sales each dollar of operating assets produces. Usually, you'll use year-end figures, although if you track your operating assets over the period of a year and average them out, your final result will be more accurate. Here's the formula:

$$\frac{\text{sales}}{\text{operating assets}}$$

If your company recorded yearly sales of $500,000 with operating assets of $100,000, it turned each asset dollar five times ($500,000/$100,000 = 5). Put another way, each dollar of assets produced five dollars of sales.

Using the figures above, the company with an operating margin of 4% and an asset turnover of 5 has an earning power ratio of 4% × 5, or 20%.

While this ratio can be compared with figures from the *Annual Statement Studies*, a more useful comparison is with your own historical earning power ratio. This is perhaps your best guide to how well your business, from an operating profit standpoint, is doing now.

Second Chance Clothing uses a worksheet to track its earning power ratio.

Figure 1–6 lists all the figures and the two component parts of the earning power ratio. For the current year, sales of $500,000 created an operating margin of $15,000, or 3% of the sales total. Each dollar of operating assets produced five dollars of sales ($100,000 in assets created $500,000 in sales). When the two figures are multiplied

```
-----------------------------------------------------------------
:                  Earning Power Worksheet                       :
:                                                                :
:  Current year                                                  :
:  ------------                                                  :
:                     Operating      Operating                   :
:            Sales    Income         Margin                      :
:            500,000  15,000         3.0 %                       :
:                                                                :
:                     ---------------------------------          :
:                                                                :
:                     Operating      Asset                       :
:            Sales    Assets         Turnover                    :
:            500,000  100,000        5.0                         :
:                                                                :
:    Earning Power Percentage: 15.0 %                            :
:    Historical average:       17.0 %                            :
:    Variance:               -  2.0 %                            :
:                                                                :
:===============================================================:
:                                                                :
:   Last year                                                    :
:   ---------                                                    :
:                     Operating      Operating                   :
:            Sales    Income         Margin                      :
:            550,000  12,000         2.2 %                       :
:                                                                :
:                     ---------------------------------          :
:                                                                :
:                     Operating      Asset                       :
:            Sales    Assets         Turnover                    :
:            550,000  75,000         7.3                         :
:                                                                :
:    Earning Power Percentage: 16.1 %                            :
:    Historical average:       17.0 %                            :
:    Variance:               -  0.9 %                            :
:                                                                :
:===============================================================:
:                                                                :
:   Upcoming year                                                :
:   -------------                                                :
:                     Operating      Operating                   :
:            Sales    Income         Margin                      :
:            [_____]  [_____]       [_____]                     :
:                                                                :
:                     ---------------------------------          :
:                                                                :
:                     Operating      Asset                       :
:            Sales    Assets         Turnover                    :
:            [_____]  [_____]       [_____]                     :
:                                                                :
:    Earning Power Percentage:    [_____]                        :
:    Historical Average:          [_____]                        :
:    Variance:                    [_____]                        :
:                                                                :
:===============================================================:
```

Figure 1-6 Earning power worksheet.

together (3% × 5), the result (15) is the business's earning power ratio during the year shown.

Fran also lists the company's historical average (it's 17%) and the variance between current figures and what the business usually records.

The center section of Figure 1–6 lists the same information for last year. Then, with higher sales, the company recorded a profit of $12,000, or 2.2% of sales. At that time, however, its operating assets were only $75,000, so each operating asset produced sales of $7.30 ($550,000/$75,000).

Because the business was able to use its assets so effectively—to create *more* sales with *less* in assets—the earning power of the company was slightly higher last year than it is for the current year.

What does this information tell Fran? First, it shows that both areas—profit as a percentage of sales, and sales divided by operating assets—have an impact on the earning power of her business. It also says that if the company could have used its assets as effectively during the current year as it did last year, sales would have been $100,000 × 7.3, or $730,000.

If this were your company, wouldn't you want to know why the operating assets of your business aren't doing as well as they did last year? Of course you would, and you'd find out the reasons by looking at each operating asset with an eye to how it's being used. You'd want to make sure you don't have equipment your people aren't familiar with, so it just sits there unused. (There are productivity worksheets in Chapter 9.) You'd check your inventory turnover rate to make sure what you bought isn't sitting on your shelves. You'd make sure dollars were flowing through your accounts receivable system instead of getting stuck there. (In Chapter 7 there's more on how you calculate your inventory turnover rate and on how to make sure your receivables move.) Above all, you must remember that once you spot a problem—in this example, operating assets that aren't producing as much in sales as they seem capable of—you need to discover why it exists and then fix it.

Tips and Guidelines

When you look at your income statement and see the gross profit your company produces, convert it into single-dollar terms. If your business recorded an average gross margin of 32% over the past year, then you've got 32 cents out of every sales dollar to pay your overhead costs.

Think of gross profit as the fund where the cash comes from to pay all your indirect (overhead) amounts, including that most important one: your own salary.

Think of net profit in the same manner. If your company recorded a net profit of 4%, think in single-dollar terms and realize that after all is said and done, for each one dollar in sales, you had four cents left. It really gives you a feel for how much—or how little—remains once everything has been paid. It helps bring the figures down to earth and makes them easier to relate to. It's especially useful when something that will increase your costs comes along. When you know you're working with pennies, controlling costs becomes more and more important.

Figure out which assets are producing profits and which are more window dressing than anything else. What have you been investing in lately? For more on how to evaluate assets—especially fixed assets—see Chapter 9.

There are other ways to examine your gross and/or net profit performance. For example, compare your net profit to the total investment you and others have made in your company. The difference tells you the return on all the capital invested in the business. From a banking standpoint, does your company deserve more of an investment? Would you lend your own business more money?

If so, consider what you'd do with the cash. Do you need it for operating expenses or to help pay long- or short-term debt? Think about what you might do with that total investment if it weren't tied up in your business. Can you get a better rate of return on that cash somewhere else?

Be sure things are categorized properly on your income statement. Too often, costs like workmen's compensation insurance are shown as an indirect (overhead) amount instead of as a direct cost. Remember that if you didn't have any direct labor, you would have no workmen's compensation insurance expense, so it should be listed under the direct cost heading. Truck insurance, though, is usually an indirect cost—you're going to pay for insurance even if all your trucks sit still.

Try to track what really happens to the profit your company makes. Does it stay in the business, or did you spend last year's profit on a vacation trip? If you did keep those dollars in the company, what did you use them for? A new vehicle or machine? If your business recorded a loss, where did the dollars come from to handle it? A loss might seem to be only a paper loss when you see it on your income statement, but it represents real money that is now no longer available to your company and must be replaced with other cash. The easiest way to track your profits and losses is with your Flow of Funds Statement, which is discussed in Chapter 3.

2

Licking the Liquidity Squeeze

Midtown Collectibles is a small but growing retail store that handles specialty ceramic figurines (including their repair and restoration), limited-edition plates, greeting cards, and so on. Midtown's liquidity problem is that its business is very seasonal; about 50% of the company's total sales come after Labor Day, with the bulk of its sales recorded from Thanksgiving to Christmas.

In effect, Midtown's owner, Courtney, faces a dual problem each holiday season: She must have enough (and the right kind of) inventory on hand, and she must hire extra help. She has to invest enough in her inventory to have adequate stock available, and it must be ordered and paid for long before her sales start to jump. At the same time, she must keep enough cash in reserve so she can pay her salespeople and other overhead expenses.

There's some seasonality—where you sell more at one time of the year than at others—in any business. But a company whose sales fluctuate widely must be especially careful in how it works with liquidity.

The Price of Not Being Liquid

Has your own business ever been in a position where it really needed to purchase something and just didn't have the cash to make the deal? Have you ever had the opportunity to make a great buy on inventory items you sell all the time but didn't have the ready cash available? Most business owners have encountered situations like these at one time or another because they're just not liquid enough at the right time. If you're good at managing liquidity, then you almost always have enough cash when you need it.

Liquidity is necessarily a function that directly relates to forecasting. If you can forecast your cash needs with some accuracy, you'll always know how liquid you need to be and exactly when.

Unfortunately, liquidity is not easy to get a handle on. First, your cash is always moving through your company, and it's sometimes difficult to know where all of it is at any given time. Second, if you allow people to charge what they buy through an accounts receivable system, you never know for sure when those outstanding amounts will be paid, so it's difficult to guess your future cash position. Nonetheless, you must develop an accurate way to forecast your cash needs.

You can ask a thousand questions about liquidity, but the bottom line is very simple: You must have the cash at the right time. Payroll this week is $4,200; if you can't cover it, you're out of business. The phone bill is $475; if your phone is shut off because you didn't mail the check, you're out of business. If you're not properly liquid at the right time, you're forced to sell long-term investments or other assets to pay your current debts. That's perhaps the cruelest cut of all: having to reduce the price of some of your merchandise so it sells quickly, thus losing the chance to make a profit, because you needed to raise cash to make a loan payment.

At the same time, you obviously can't keep all of your dollars in cash. If they're not out working for you as inventory and labor and trucks and equipment and machinery, you would be out of business, and perhaps for a worse reason: You didn't let your money do its job for your company.

Balancing Cash and Costs

What's the solution? To know how much cash you need and when you can expect to collect it and to have any leftover dollars out working for you in the best possible way. There are obvious budget connections to your liquidity position (which are detailed in Chapter 11), and at the same time, there are a few rules of thumb that can help you understand and forecast your liquidity condition.

The best way to prevent liquidity problems is to have enough cash available, before you even start your company, to handle any liquidity situation you might get yourself into. Unfortunately, not many small businesses have an excess of capital; in fact, most don't have enough. Furthermore, the dollars you have to work with are always moving, both in and out (often more seem to go out than in), so the amount of cash you have available at any particular time varies. Normally you'd say a business that collects exactly what it spends has broken even, and in profit terms that would be correct. But from a liquidity standpoint things get more complex, as bills and the cash to pay them never seem to arrive at the same time.

Figure 2-1 details Midtown Collectible's sales, gross expenses, and profit before taxes over a twelve-month period. For the first third of the year, Courtney's small business recorded a decent monthly profit. As her buying picked up slightly during the summer months, she spent exactly the same as what she took in. Starting in August, as she began to buy for the fall season—the time she'll record the bulk of her sales—she had to survive three months of huge deficits. Her inventory purchases far outweighed the dollars that came into her store. Finally, during the last two months of the year, Midtown Collectibles moved back into the profit column once again, with the figures more than making up for the losses it suffered during August, September, and October.

For many business owners a picture like Figure 2-1 causes havoc in terms of liquidity. Without some cash in reserve, the business— even if it saves all the profits it made during the first third of the

```
:----------------------------------------------------------------:
:                                                                :
:            Expenses    Sales   Sales - Expenses                :
:                                                                :
:   Jan         8000     10000        2000                       :
:   Feb         8000     10000        2000                       :
:   Mar         8000     10000        2000                       :
:   Apr         8000     10000        2000                       :
:   May        10000     10000          0                        :
:   Jun        10000     10000          0                        :
:   Jul        10000     10000          0                        :
:   Aug        15000     10000       -5000                       :
:   Sep        20000     15000       -5000                       :
:   Oct        25000     15000      -10000                       :
:   Nov        10000     20000       10000                       :
:   Dec        10000     25000       15000                       :
:             -----------------------------------                :
:   Totals    142000    155000       13000                       :
:----------------------------------------------------------------:
```

Figure 2-1 Worksheet showing expenses, sales, sales—expenses.

year—will run out of funds before the end of September. In effect, it will need a cash transfusion in September, some outside cash to get it through until November's money arrives.

Midtown Collectibles ended up with a profit before taxes of $13,000. Let's assume the company paid taxes at a 40% rate, leaving it with about $8,000 in the bank to use toward the following year. Does that put it in good enough condition to handle next year's fluctuations in sales and costs?

If conditions stay exactly the same for Midtown Collectibles—if sales and costs remain identical to those recorded during the previous year—how will Courtney do from a liquidity standpoint? Here's what her cash balance will look like during the first third of the year:

(from last year)	$ 8,000
January	$10,000
February	$12,000
March	$14,000
April	$16,000

Courtney's built a strong cash reserve, ready to be used as she heads into the summer break-even period. The next third of the year looks like this:

May	$16,000
June	$16,000
July	$16,000
August	$11,000

August's purchases cut a deep slice out of Courtney's cash position, but she still has nearly all of last year's profit to work with as she heads into her busiest buying/selling season. Here's the last third of her year:

September	$ 6,000
October	($ 4,000)
November	$ 6,000
December	$21,000

Even with a year in business behind her, Courtney still needs more cash than she's made, if she's to pay her expenses during October. She needs less than what she had to come up with during the previous year (Midtown Collectibles was $12,000 behind last October), but she's still short of funds.

To find the dollars she needs, perhaps Courtney can invest more of her own money into the business or get some outside investors to put money into the company. If not, she'll have to arrange a bank loan—preferably before she's out of cash—to handle the shortfall.

Forecasting Your Cash Needs

Sometimes a chart makes a series of numbers more understandable, so Courtney spends the time it takes to plot her sales and cost information. That gives her a visual image of what's happening to her company.

Figure 2–2 plots the data from Figure 2–1. As noted, the line marked with plus signs (+) charts the sales figures, while the line marked with small boxes plots the company's expenses. Whenever cash exceeds costs, there's a surplus (and vice versa). During the early months plotted in this example, cash came in at a higher rate than costs were recorded, so Courtney had a surplus in her cash account. Starting in May, her business collected exactly the same amount as

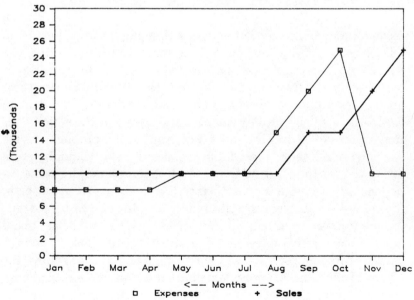

Figure 2–2   Sales vs. expenses line graph, showing one gap.

it spent, so both lines ran together for a time. By the end of August, costs began to exceed the cash collected. The gap in the two lines shows the severity of Midtown Collectable's liquidity problem.

For this particular business, the liquidity difficulties are caused by a dependence on seasonal sales, but patterns like the one shown in this graph can occur for many reasons. For example, say a company records a sharp increase in sales. Such huge jumps are hard to predict and difficult for a company to handle. But to be successful, business owners must accurately predict their sales, and they can do this by reviewing records and carefully monitoring sales trends. A construction business, for example, can count on selling a certain percentage of the estimates it provides. If the value of those estimates takes a sharp jump, then the business owner can figure that sales will follow and increase at about the same rate. If a retail business has shown increased sales every month for the past six or seven months, it will probably continue to rise at about the same rate. If a wholesale company's business has been increasing, and it's approaching what's usually the best season of the year, it's a pretty safe bet sales will boom.

The Time Lag Between Sales and Payments

As you know, there's almost always a time lag between when you sell something and when you get paid for it. In the meantime, you have to pay your employees, and often you must pay for at least part of the materials and equipment you used for the work. During those good times, your cash often flows out much faster than it comes in. Cash inflow will eventually catch up and overcome the deficit position, of course, but in the meantime, you have a problem.

Figure 2–2 shows that Midtown Collectibles had liquidity problems only one time during the year. Most companies, however, experience several periods when their costs exceed their incoming cash. Figure 2–3 illustrates such a situation, picturing two cash gaps during the twelve-month period shown. The gaps in the chart detail exactly when the company had liquidity problems. To have enough cash to work against the times where costs exceed cash inflow, the owner of this business must marshall all available sources of cash and save every penny possible when things are good.

The company in this chart shows the same bottom line that Midtown Collectibles did: a profit before taxes of $13,000. Anyone who

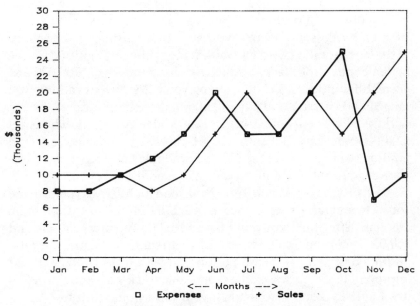

Figure 2–3 Sales vs. expenses line graph, showing two gaps.

just looks at the end result will miss the liquidity difficulty the company in Figure 2–3 finds itself in from April through June and again in October.

Current Assets and Your Operating Cycle

To prevent liquidity problems, you must calculate your *current assets*—cash and those items you can expect to convert into cash within a reasonable time. Current assets includes things like your inventory, which you plan to sell and thus convert into cash, and your accounts receivable, which you expect to collect, both within your next operating cycle. Basically, your *operating cycle* is the time it takes your business to make a sale, get the items to the customer (delivered or installed), and to collect for the sale.

Most business owners, when they talk about current assets, immediately think of what a banker calls the *current ratio*, which compares current assets to current liabilities. *Working capital*—the amount of cash you have to do business with—also comes from these two figures. The difference between your current assets and current liabilities equals your working capital. (There's more information on working capital in Chapter 3 and on current ratios in Chapter 4.)

While it's important to track your current ratio performance, from a liquidity standpoint it's necessary to understand that a change in the current ratio doesn't always change your cash position for the better. For example, let's say you have current assets of $100,000 and current liabilities of $50,000, giving you a 2:1 current ratio. If you take $10,000 in cash and pay $10,000 in those liabilities, you're left with $90,000 in current assets and $40,000 in current liabilities—a 2.25:1 current ratio. But at the same time you've weakened your cash position (you don't have the $10,000 available any longer). So while your current ratio is higher, your cash condition is poorer.

If you take out a short-term bank loan for $10,000, you increase your current assets and your current liabilities—by that same amount. After the loan you'd have $110,000 in current assets and $60,000 in current liabilities, or a 1.8:1 current ratio. While your ratio position dropped, your cash position (at least for the moment) has improved. If you borrowed the same money on a long-term basis (say it was due 18 months from now), your ratio would shift to 2.2:1, as your current liabilities aren't affected (you'd have $110,000 in current assets divided by $50,000 in current liabilities). The point is, while ratio analysis is useful, it doesn't necessarily reflect how liquid your assets are.

Putting Working Capital in the Right Place

It's easy to confuse working capital with liquidity, too, but they're not the same. As mentioned earlier, your total working capital is calculated by subtracting your current liabilities from your current assets. Working capital is easier to understand when it's compared with other things in your business, such as sales or assets, than it is just as a raw total. As an example, let's look at two businesses with the same working capital:

	Hometown Auto	A-1 Brake Service
Current Assets	100,000	200,000
Current Liabilities	60,000	160,000
Working Capital	40,000	40,000

Hometown Auto and A-1 Brake Service are clearly not in the same position from a standpoint of financial strength. Current liabilities for Hometown Auto come to 60% of current assets, while for A-1 Brake Service they're 80%. Which company would you rather loan money to?

It's also important to note that while you almost always think of working capital as cash, it never is in a completely liquid form. You use it for inventory, to pay your employees while you wait for your customers to pay you, and so on.

Figure 2–4, a column chart, plots the working capital of Midtown Collectibles as a percentage of its total sales. For the first eight months of the year, the company's working capital was about 40% of sales or higher. Starting in September, the percentage figure started dropping and continued to decrease throughout the rest of the year. This picture is consistent with what the business should expect—as it gets into the time of the year when its sales really jump, working capital as a percentage of those sales will naturally decrease.

There's no great danger to this situation unless market conditions change and business takes a turn for the worse. Since each dollar of working capital is now producing more sales, Courtney knows

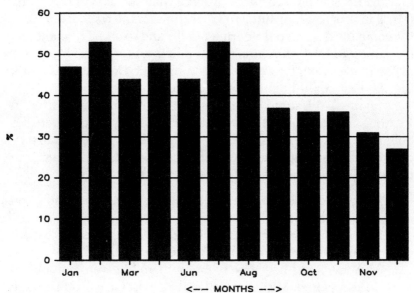

Figure 2–4 Column chart for working capital as a percentage of sales.

```
!---------------------------------------------------------------!
!                                                               !
!              Working capital worksheet for June               !
!                                                               !
!  Total current assets:          65,000                        !
!  Total current liabilities:     17,000                        !
!                                 --------                       !
!                                                               !
!    Current working capital      48,000                        !
!                                                               !
!                                                               !
!    Locations:                   Amount      Percentage        !
!                                                               !
!    Cash:                         3,696         7.7 %           !
!    Accounts receivable:         18,000        37.5 %           !
!    Inventory:                   12,480        26.0 %           !
!    Work in progress:            13,824        28.8 %           !
!    [_____]       [_____]    [_____% ]          !
!    [_____]       [_____]    [_____% ]          !
!    [_____]       [_____]    [_____% ]          !
!    [_____]       [_____]    [_____% ]          !
!                                                               !
!---------------------------------------------------------------!
```

Figure 2-5   Working capital worksheet for June.

it's even more important than usual to make sure her cash is where she wants it to be.

Figure 2–5 is a worksheet that you can use to determine where your working capital happens to be at any given time. In this case, Courtney finds that she's not really strong in the cash department, with less than 8% of her funds in the form of cash. She also has more invested in the work she has in progress than she does in inventory. (Work in progress for Midtown Collectibles is the restoration work the company does on old figurines, dolls, and so on.) The company has almost $14,000 that hasn't been billed yet (or it would appear as part of the accounts receivable total). In effect, Courtney has nearly $14,000 that could be put to better use.

Figure 2–6 is a pie chart that plots the information listed in Figure 2–5. This makes it even easier for Courtney to see where her dollars are, to really get a feel for the numbers. When Courtney discovered how much cash was invested in work in progress, she checked her work orders and discovered several reasons:

1. Some of the jobs were waiting for parts that had been ordered.
2. Some of her work was done and the customers had called, but the work hadn't been picked up or billed.
3. A few items had time spent on them but were not able to be repaired. Midtown Collectibles most likely won't be able to charge its customers for this work.

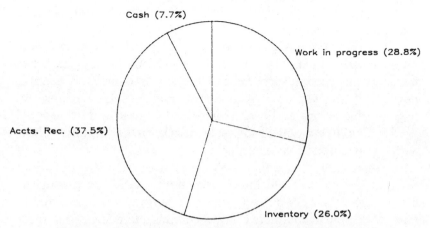

Figure 2-6 Pie chart showing location of working capital.

4. Some of the work needed parts ordered, but for one reason or another, they hadn't been.
5. Some of the work could be finished quickly (and the customers billed for it), but Courtney's employees were working on other projects.

The last item in Courtney's list is probably the one many small businesses run up against the most. Often you'll find yourself having to choose between two jobs to do: one that you can complete and will bring in a substantial sum of cash as soon as you do, and another that you will only be able to partly finish, which means that you won't be able to bill the customer for the work. The problem is that the customer with the job you won't be able to complete is usually the one who yells the loudest, which leads you you to do the work for him.

Courtney also discovered that much of the work her business had in progress could be partly billed. By sending her customers a bill for "work to date," she was able to collect some of these dollars.

Knowing the Length of Your Operating Cycle

Once Courtney has a good idea of where her working capital is, she needs to calculate how much of it is truly liquid. Her current assets are composed of cash, marketable securities, notes due her within one year (or operating cycle), work in progress, inventory, and accounts receivable. Cash is obviously liquid, and you'd expect that marketable securities are, too.

Knowing the length of your operating cycle is important for several reasons. First, it's the time when you expect sitting assets like inventory and accounts receivable to be converted into cash. Second, during this time you'll pay all of your current obligations, and you must be able to forecast how much cash you'll need and when you'll need it. Finally, your operating cycle is the key to understanding how cash moves through your business.

Most people figure that their operating cycle is usually about one year, and if it isn't calculated, accountants use the one-year figure. But that isn't always correct, for each business takes a different amount of time to complete its average transaction (e.g., from making the sale to ordering the equipment and parts for the job or from doing the work and collecting from the customer). To calculate your operating cycle, add your average collection period to your inventory turnover rate.

Your *average collection period* is the usual time it takes you to collect for your sales once you've recorded them into your accounts receivable system. This figure is easy to calculate; just go back over your books and average your month-ending accounts receivable totals for the period you want to look at. For this example, let's say they average $30,000.

You also must know your credit sales figure: how much you charged through your accounts receivable system during the year. Let's say it came to $360,000.

If you divide your total yearly credit sales ($360,000) by your average accounts receivable total ($30,000), you get an answer of 12. This means that you generated and collected money through your receivable system 12 times during this year. When you divide the 365 days in the year by 12, you know you've got an average collection period of 30.4 days. That's right on target if you sell to your customers on a net-30 day basis. But if you ask for and expect payment within 10 days after you bill them, a 30-day collection period means you have liquidity problems.

Furthermore, if you sell on a net-30 basis and buy on the same terms, you and your suppliers get paid only if everyone pays on time. If your customers don't pay you until, say, 45 days after they're billed, you won't be able to pay your own bills on time.

You must have even more liquidity if some of the people you buy from offer trade discounts to your company. Many wholesalers offer a discount if they're paid by the tenth of the month following the purchase. Obviously, if your customers don't send you a check until after the tenth of the month, you won't be able to take advantage of these discounts. The easiest solution to this problem, and one that will improve your liquidity immediately, is to offer your own discount to customers who pay by the fifth (or whatever day will allow you to take a discount when you pay your own invoices; give yourself a few days leeway).

The second thing that makes up your average operating cycle is your *inventory turnover rate*, a measure of how fast your inventory, on average, is sold and taken out of your stock. You can calculate this rate for any period of time, but to keep it simple, let's work with yearly figures. Let's say that your cost of goods sold figure (from your balance sheet) is $150,000. Let's also assume that you carry an average inventory of $50,000.

If you divide the cost of goods sold ($150,000) by the average inventory ($50,000), you get an answer of 3. This means you turned your inventory an average of 3 times during the year, and when you divide 365 (days) by 3, you know you moved your inventory, on average, every 122 days.

When you add your average collection period (30.4 days) to your average inventory turnover period (122 days), you learn that your business had an average operating cycle of about 152 days, or roughly, five months.

Evaluating Current Assets

Courtney, whose small company came up with the same data, now knows how to evaluate her assets. They're only current if they'll be converted into cash within one operating cycle—in her case, within the next five months or so.

Courtney needs to look at her securities with an eye to their marketability. Sure, she might be able to sell them quickly, but would she do so, during the next five months, if their value had dropped significantly from what she had paid for them? Probably not—so any securities whose prices have lowered should not be listed as a current asset but as a long-term investment.

The same holds true for any notes that Courtney expects to collect within the operating cycle. How confident is she that the note(s) will be paid during this time?

Of course, Courtney's inventory isn't completely liquid, as she doesn't know when she'll sell what she has in stock, nor will she sell everything she has on hand. Her accounts receivable also aren't 100% liquid because she doesn't know when people will pay what they owe her.

To summarize, you must include in your current assets only those accounts receivable that you really expect to collect. Figure your total inventory value as current only if it will be sold during the next year or operating cycle. Don't include any stocks or other securities unless they're really something you'd sell within that same period.

The Cash Ratio and the Quick Ratio

The *cash ratio* takes a harsher look at your business's liquidity by comparing what you have in cash or cash equivalents with your total current assets. This lets you know how much of your working capital is currently in a purely liquid form. The cash ratio lets you see how much of your total current assets (made up of cash, notes due, your inventory, and your accounts receivable) are liquid. The higher this ratio, the more liquid your current asset group. For instance, two businesses might show these figures:

	Hometown Auto	A-1 Brake Service
Cash and cash equivalents	12,000	6,000
Current assets	24,000	24,000

Hometown Auto is 50% liquid—half of its current assets are in cash or its equivalent. A-1 Brake Service has only 25% of its current assets in the form of cash or cash equivalents.

The cash ratio tells you how much of your current asset base is available to pay current obligations. If you follow your own cash ratio over time, you'll soon find out what percentage is right for you. Here's how. If your current obligations average 60% of your normal current assets, then you know you must somehow keep 60% (or more) of those assets in a liquid form. If you don't, you won't be able to pay your bills when they come due, so you'll have to stretch out their payment schedule until you can convert some other assets into cash.

That often causes worse problems, especially if the condition persists over a period of time. You end up paying on bills that are four or five months old, while your current obligations are themselves aging every day.

Another useful ratio, called the *quick ratio* or *acid test*, gives you an instant picture of how your current cash condition compares with the total of your current liabilities. You can compute your quick ratio by dividing your total cash and cash equivalents by your current liabilities. (Cash and cash equivalents do not include your inventory and accounts receivable.) You might end up with something like this:

Cash and cash equivalents	42,000
Current liabilities	37,000
Quick ratio	1.14:1

This is something like comparing the bills you have to pay this week with the paycheck you just cashed. Most people feel a 1:1 ratio is desirable, but like everything else, your quick ratio will vary according to the way you operate your company. Track your quick ratio over a period of time and watch for a variation, particularly one that shows your cash position getting weaker.

The Best Level of Liquidity for Your Business

Why not create a graph that plots your liquidity along with the profit or loss your company recorded? You might learn that your business is the most profitable when it has 75% of its current assets in a liquid form (and thus can respond swiftly when special purchases come along, take advantage of cash discounts, and so on). This percentage figure could be anything, of course; the idea is to determine what's best for you.

You may discover that your company works best with a low level of liquidity: You must have your cash out working for you all the time instead of sitting in the bank.

Once you learn the best level of liquidity for your business, try to stretch it to the limit in terms of maintaining the proper level. For example, if you seem to be the most successful with a lot of liquidity, try to change your operation so that you always are very liquid.

You might also consider if your money is earning all the interest it can. If you accurately forecast the cash needs of your business, you'll be able to move your dollars around so they're most profitable.

Before you make any major purchase, consider its effect on your liquidity over the next year. If you spend a certain sum this month to buy something, that money won't be available at least until the new investment starts to create a return. How will today's removal of cash affect your cash position in three months or a year?

When does most of the money flow into your business? More often than not, it's during the first ten days of the month, but check your bank deposits for the past year or so to make sure. Take it a step further and compare the cash you receive with your prior month-end accounts receivable total. What's the average percentage? If you can get a line on this figure, you'll be able to make a pretty accurate estimate of how much you'll collect the following month.

3

The Critical Balance: Cash Flow and Debt

Skyline Nursery is a typical small business, perhaps one with a larger investment in inventory than many but with all the same problems every small company has. Skyline handles what you'd expect a nursery to—trees and plants and such—and Skyline's owner, Val, also has a retail florist connected to her nursery, as well as a landscaping and gardening service. That means Val's labor costs are more significant than they would be if the company was just in the nursery business.

From a cash flow/debt standpoint, it means that Val has supplier bills to pay as well as a payroll (and its associated taxes) to meet every week. If her cash flow dams up for some reason, Val's got problems.

Like many business owners, Val finds maintaining the proper balance between cash flow and debt something like walking a tightrope: wonderful if you can do it but not much fun while you're up there.

Too often, the business owner thinks of debt as something that must be paid in the future (as in *long-term* debt) or as a bank loan that's due next month (when the business should have more money). It's thought of as a loan, rather than as just what its name says it is: *debt*. When you think of your cash in relation to your debts, you should consider everything you owe and when it's due to be paid.

The relationship between a company's cash flow and its debt is basically the same regardless of the type of business you happen to be in. If you sell everything on a purely retail, cash-and-carry basis, there will be times when you must pay for the inventory purchases while the products you bought are still sitting on your shelves. That's the way with anyone who buys in hundreds but sells one at a time: There's a time lag between when you have to pay for what you bought and when you sell (and get paid for) it. Ideally, your business will create enough sales volume so that your monthly cash collections will be more than the money you owe your suppliers.

If you let some of your customers charge at least part of what they buy from you, there's always a delay between the time you mail the invoice and when you get your check. During this period, you often have to pay your employees for labor and your suppliers for materials that were purchased by your customer.

If you're in the wholesale business, you not only deal with larger sales and costs volumes but also always have accounts receivable that arrive slower than your payments go out. Many wholesalers offer discounts to encourage prompt payment, but there always seem to be some customers who just never pay when they promise they will.

Understanding Depreciation

Cash flow is usually defined as the profit your business made plus the depreciation that it recorded over a period of time. *Depreciation* is an estimate of how much an asset decreased in value over a specific period. The trucks and machinery and other equipment you own often become less productive as time goes on, or they require more maintenance expense, or they become outmoded, so they're simply worth less each year—at least from an accounting standpoint. Depreciation isn't a cash savings as such, as it's only a paper transaction, but it saves you money at tax time.

When you first purchase any fixed asset that the law allows you to depreciate, your accountant sets up a depreciation schedule that lists the purchase price, any salvage value (an estimate of what the asset will be worth when it's fully depreciated), and a schedule that lists each year's depreciation over the estimated life of the asset. You might buy a new truck, for example, for $12,000. Your accountant might estimate that after five years—the period of time this vehicle can be depreciated—the truck will have a salvage value of $2,000. That means that each year, $2,000 will be depreciated. (A total price of $12,000 less $2,000 salvage value leaves $10,000; $10,000 divided by five years gives you $2,000 per year in depreciation.)

It's important to note that depreciation is *not* accumulated cash that's available to buy a new truck (or whatever) once the old one's been depreciated. Any new purchase must be paid from the cash the business generates. *Accumulated depreciation* (listed on your balance sheet for each asset) is just a listing of the cost of the portion of the asset that has been charged to depreciation.

To understand how depreciation works and what a difference it can make to Skyline Nursery, Val put some figures into a worksheet.

Figure 3–1 details two sets of numbers for Skyline Nursery: One that shows no depreciation and another that lists $3,000 in depreciation for the year.

If no depreciation is recorded, the business has a higher profit before taxes, pays more in income tax, and has a higher after-tax profit, too, at least on paper. Here, the business records an after-tax profit of $12,960.

Cash flow is lower, though, by about $1,000. It's reduced by the amount of the effective tax rate (here, 28% is used for the sake of illustration) multiplied by the amount of depreciation. The actual cash flow when $3,000 in depreciation is recorded is the net profit of $10,800 plus the depreciation—a total of $13,800.

Since the IRS is constantly changing the rules for how depreciation is calculated, this book isn't the place to detail how your business should handle it. Ask your accountant. The point here is that depreciation adds directly to the cash flow your business records because of the tax savings it allows. However, when you depreciate

```
!--------------------------------------------------------------------!
! (without depreciation)          !    (with depreciation)           !
!                                 !                                  !
!Net Sales                400,000 !  Net Sales                400,000 !
!Direct costs             280,000 !  Direct costs             280,000 !
!Other               [_____]    !  Other               [_____]  !
!                                 !                                  !
!Total direct costs       280,000 !  Total direct costs       280,000 !
!                                 !                                  !
!Overhead                  92,000 !  Overhead                  92,000 !
!Other costs               10,000 !  Other costs               10,000 !
!Depreciation                   0 !  Depreciation               3,000 !
!                                 !                                  !
!Net profit before taxes   18,000 !  Net profit before taxes   15,000 !
!                                 !                                  !
!Taxes at 28%               5,040 !  Taxes at 28%               4,200 !
!                                 !                                  !
!Net profit after taxes    12,960 !  Net profit after taxes    10,800 !
!                                 !                                  !
!Net + depreciation        12,960 !  Net + depreciation        13,800 !
!                        ========= !                        ========= !
!                                 !                                  !
!--------------------------------------------------------------------!
```

Figure 3–1   Depreciation worksheet.

something, you're more often than not making payments on it at the same time, so these dollars enter into the equation, too.

Calculating Your Cash Flow

Profit plus depreciation equals cash flow is the the textbook definition of cash flow, but more and more business managers are changing the way they view the subject, as it's affected by the debt a business has. In Figure 3-1, the calculated cash flow for Skyline Nursery, assuming it recorded $3,000 in depreciation, was $13,800.

But what's the business depreciating? Are there payments to be made on the equipment or machinery or building? Probably so, so that part of Skyline's cash flow is already spoken for, already earmarked to make the payments.

So a better definition of cash flow would be the cash that's left on hand after each expense, including all the payments you've promised to make, has been paid.

You calculate the cash flow for your business like this:

Cash balance, start of the month		$17,000
+ Cash received during the month	+	23,000
− Cash paid out during the month	−	20,000
Cash on hand, end of month		$20,000

You can create a worksheet that calculates your expected cash flow over a period of time in much the same way that you prepare a budget worksheet.

Val put together one for Skyline Nursery based on several assumptions. The business will collect for about 95% of what it sells, and it will let its customers charge what they buy through an accounts receivable system. Material costs are calculated at 43% of sales, direct labor at 22% of sales, and overhead is figured at 23% of sales.

Figure 3-2 is a bare-bones cash worksheet that starts with a zero beginning balance and runs for six months. Because of the amount of cash actually collected, Val can look at this worksheet and know that her company—if the projections are correct—will have made a profit of about 5% at the end of the period. But she'll have to worry about her cash position in February, when she'll be $4,200 short. If Val keeps what the business earned for the prior month, she'll need only $1,100 to take care of February's cash deficit.

:Cash budget worksheet - first six months

		JAN	FEB	MAR	APR	MAY	JUN	JUL	AUG
Sales:		30,000	40,000	35,000	30,000	37,000	35,000	[ ]	[ ]
Cash received:		28,500	31,000	32,000	34,000	34,000	28,500	[ ]	[ ]
Loans:		[ ]	[ ]	[ ]	[ ]	[ ]	[ ]	[ ]	[ ]
Other:		[ ]	[ ]	[ ]	[ ]	[ ]	[ ]	[ ]	[ ]
Total cash inflow:		28,500	31,000	32,000	34,000	34,000	28,500	[ ]	[ ]
Cash outflow:									
Material costs:	43.00%	12,900	17,200	15,050	12,900	15,910	15,050		
Direct labor costs:	22.00%	6,600	8,800	7,700	6,600	8,140	7,700		
Overhead:	23.00%	6,900	9,200	8,050	6,900	8,510	8,050		
Other:									
Total cash outflow:		26,400	35,200	30,800	26,400	32,560	30,800		
Starting cash balance:		0	2,600	(1,100)	600	8,700	10,640		
Cash inflow:		2,100	(4,200)	1,200	7,600	1,440	(2,300)		
Depreciation:		500	500	500	500	500	500		
Ending cash balance:		2,600	(1,100)	600	8,700	10,640	8,840		

Figure 3-2 Cash budget worksheet.

The idea here is that Val at least knows when there will be a cash shortfall in the business and can plan for it before it arrives. Obviously, it's always a good idea to have a loan arranged before the day you need the money.

Sources and Uses of Funds

To really help prevent cash difficulties caused by your own specific cash flow/debt balance, you need to know where each dollar in your business comes from and where each dollar goes. One of the ways to track this is by using the *Flow of Funds* statement that your accountant gives you. At first glance, this isn't the easiest form to understand, but it's often the most useful.

This statement, also called the *Statement of Sources and Uses of Funds,* the *Statement of Change in Financial Position,* and the *Statement of Sources and Application of Funds,* is designed to show where your cash came from, and where it went, over the period under examination.

One difficulty with this form is that the terms used to describe the movement of your dollars are often confusing. Consider, for instance, your inventory. If your business, over a specific period, increased its investment in the stock you have on hand, it can be said that you used funds. In fact, you did, because you put some of your cash into those products you have in stock. If you show an increase in your accounts receivable total, that means you also used funds there, as it's taken more of the cash you have available to support the purchases you let customers charge. From an accounting standpoint, if you have more money in the bank at the end of one period than you did at the end of the last period, you've used funds. Used in the accounting sense doesn't mean the dollars are gone, but rather that they've been put in an exact location.

On the other hand, if you lower the amount of your inventory, you've created a *source* of funds. You didn't just give the products away, but rather sold them, and thus increased the dollars your business has available. You converted some sitting funds into cash, turning them into a source of dollars for your business. If you lower your investment in accounts receivable, you also create a source of funds, because you don't have so much of your working cash collected there, functioning as a loan to some of your customers.

Liabilities operate in exactly the opposite way as assets. For example, when you increase the total in your accounts payable, you've provided a source of funds. Say your business purchases $20,000 worth of products, and your supplier lets you charge that total, giving your business $20,000 worth of goods to work with until the payment comes due. In a very real sense you've created funds, because when those items are sold, they bring dollars into your business. Once you receive and have to pay the invoice for the products you purchased, then you've lost this source of funds, but until then, you're working with someone else's money.

If you owe a short-term note and pay it off, then you've used funds, because you used some of your cash to pay the loan.

If you pay an accounts payable invoice, that lowers the total you have in accounts payable, so you've again used some funds.

To recap, if you increase an asset account (things like cash or accounts receivable or inventory), that means a use of funds has occurred, as you've tied up more cash. If you lower an asset account, that frees money, which means you've created a source of funds. When you increase a liability account, you create a source of funds, because you have more money (or products) to work with. If you take out a short-term loan, for example, you have the cash to make more money for your company. While it might seem contradictory to call liabilities sources of assets, it really is correct. If you decrease a liability by, for example, paying a bill, you have less cash, so you've used some of your funds.

The terms *source* and *use* are designed to identify where your dollars are moving. For example, you use cash by putting it somewhere, such as inventory. In this case, you no longer have access to it: It won't return to your business in the form of cash until you sell and collect for the products you have for sale. When you buy something from a wholesaler, you increase the stock you have available for sale, which will bring more cash into your company, so in essence you've created a source of funds.

To make Skyline Nursery's sources and uses of funds a bit clearer, Val created a worksheet.

Figure 3–3 classifies all sources and uses of funds as positive or negative, so everything balances. Here, the worksheet focuses on current assets and current liabilities, but it can be extended to cover other balance sheet information you might want to examine. Data is shown for two quarters of the current year.

```
!-----------------------------------------------------------------!
!                    Last      This     Source      Use           !
!                    Quarter   Quarter  of funds   of funds       !
!                                                                 !
!Current assets:                                                  !
!                                                                 !
!Cash                 8,000    6,000    (2,000)          0 !
!Inventory           40,000   35,000    (5,000)          0 !
!Accounts Receivable 30,000   40,000         0     10,000 !
![_____]  [_____] [_____] [_____] [_____]  !
![_____]  [_____] [_____] [_____] [_____]  !
!                                                                 !
!Total current assets:                  (7,000)    10,000 !
!-----------------------------------------------------------------!
!Current liabilities:                                             !
!                                                                 !
!Accounts Payable    38,000   40,000     2,000          0 !
!Short-term note due  5,000        0         0    (5,000) !
![_____]  [_____] [_____] [_____] [_____]  !
![_____]  [_____] [_____] [_____] [_____]  !
!                                                                 !
!Total                                                            !
!Current liabilities:                    2,000    (5,000) !
!                                                                 !
!-----------------------------------------------------------------!
```

Figure 3–3 Asset/liability source of funds worksheet.

The first listing is cash, which decreased $2,000 from the last quarter to this one. This creates a source of funds, as that cash is free to do other things; it's no longer stuck in the cash account. The $2,000 difference appears as a source of funds, as a negative figure, because Skyline Nursery deducted $2,000 from its cash balance to use somewhere else.

Inventory also dropped, by $5,000, from the last quarter. That, too, is a source of funds, as Skyline Nursery now has $5,000 less in its inventory account that can be put to another use at the end of the current quarter.

Val's accounts receivable increased from $30,000 to $40,000. The $10,000 difference represents a use of funds, as these dollars have been used as customer loans and are no longer available for other purposes.

Moving to the liability accounts, you'll see that Val's accounts payable increased from $38,000 to $40,000 during this period. The $2,000 increase represents a source of funds, as Val has $2,000 more of other people's money to work with.

During the two quarters, Val paid off a short-term $5,000 loan, which shows up just as you would expect—a use of funds, as the cash was spent.

For Val's liability accounts, sources of funds show as positive figures, while uses of funds are listed with parentheses around them to indicate they are negative amounts. Val can see, through this worksheet, exactly where her funds moved. When you design a worksheet for your own company, make it fit the level of detail that's useful to you. That's the real key to funds control: to focus on the information in a way that's beneficial to you.

Working Capital and Sales

In every company, there's a precise relationship between working capital and sales. Too little working capital restricts sales; too much means the business isn't using its cash efficiently. How do you measure the proper balance between the two?

With a little delving into your past history, you can determine that when working capital drops below a specific percentage of sales, those sales start to drop too.

To calculate your working capital, subtract your current liabilities from your current assets. In other words, figure out how much cash you have on hand or expect to have within the next year or operating cycle, as well as how much cash you'll need to pay the bills that are due within the same period. The difference is the cash you have to work with, your working capital.

How much working capital does your business require to support the sales volume you need just to break even? Each business starts with an exact amount of working capital. When Val started Skyline Nursery, she made the entire investment into the business: $60,000. Some of these funds went for getting the firm up and running, but most were allocated to acquiring inventory for the company's nursery division. Val figures the company spent about $10,000 in start-up costs, which left it with some $50,000 in working capital.

Since Val buys at wholesale and sells at retail, she must calculate her supportable sales by adding her markup to her available working capital. Val marks things up 30%, so $50,000 divided by .70 = $71,429. If Val put all her working capital into inventory, it would have a retail value of $71,429.

If the company sold everything it had in stock during the year, and never replenished its inventory, Val could say the business turned its working capital one time. In the real world, of course, that's not what happens. You buy new inventory when the old is sold, so over the course of a year, a business turns its working capital several times. The more you can turn it, the more profit your company will record.

The industry standard for the sales/working capital ratio for the business you're in is listed in the *Annual Statement Studies*, so you can compare your own results with those of others in your line of work. Here, markup is not used in the calculations; sales are compared with the business's net working capital.

To take things a step further, consider the other part of the equation that affects the amount of sales your working capital can support: your markup. If two companies each have $50,000 in working capital, and each turns that capital eight times per year, you'd expect they'd have the same sales/working capital ratio: 8:1.

If sales were exactly eight times working capital, that would be true. However, since working capital is calculated at cost and sales are figured on a *retail* basis, the addition of a markup figure puts both figures on the same footing. In this case, if one business marked up goods an average of 36% while the other marked them up 30%, each business has a different retail starting point:

Business A (36% markup)	Business B (30% markup)
$50,000 / .64 = $78,125	$50,000 / .70 = $71,429

If both businesses turn their marked-up working capital eight times, business A would total sales of $625,000, while business B would record sales of $571,432.

There's nothing incorrect about using working capital in its raw form and making the comparison with total sales. That lets you compare your ratio with that of other businesses in your industry and in fact is the comparison that most business owners look at. The idea here is to take things a step further and include your average markup in the calculations, so that both your working capital and your sales are on the same retail basis.

Skyline Nursery's Sales/Working Capital Ratio

During each month of that first year, Skyline Nursery paid its overhead—electricity, phone, water, and so on—and replenished its stock. At the end of its first year in business, the firm's original investment had grown slightly, to $65,000, and it had recorded sales of $500,000.

With working capital of $50,000 and sales of $500,000, Skyline Nursery has a sales/working capital ratio of 7:1. Its original retail inventory of $71,429 had produced sales of $500,000; $500,000/$71,429 = 7. That's the number of times Val's working capital turned during the year.

The importance of this information is that it tells Val the amount of business the company is doing with its working capital. It's crucial to know this, as while a firm may do less business (depending on economic conditions), its working capital limits the maximum it can do. In other words, if Skyline Nursery has $50,000 in working capital at all times, and the first-year ratio is correct, the most business it will be able to do over a yearly period is about $500,000.

Consider your own business for a moment. You can always sell less (for any number of reasons), but can you sell more? What happens if you get a real spurt in sales? Your working capital will stretch, but only so far; it will eventually reach a point where you simply won't be able to support any more sales without some outside cash. That might come from a short-term loan, or perhaps you'll sell stock in the firm, put more of your own cash into the company, and so on. The point is that a specific amount of working capital can support only an equally specific dollar volume of sales.

Consider how your company, without any outside financial help, might do an additional 15% in business over the next few months. You'd have to pay labor and material costs about 15% higher than what you've been paying. Your overhead might remain about the same, but your direct costs would increase in direct proportion to your sales. If there's a time lag between when you have to pay your costs and when you collect for the sale, you'll have a cash problem. Again, your working capital, stretched to its limit, will not support any more sales.

Here's an example: Let's say you average $60,000 in sales each month. Out of that, your direct costs come to 75%, or $45,000. If you record that 15% rise in sales, your monthly sales volume will increase to $69,000. Your direct costs will also rise, to $51,750, meaning that the amount of cash you need to pay your direct costs has also gone up 15%. As a result, you'll need an extra $6,750 in cash every month just to pay your direct costs. At least some of the increase in sales will start to come back into your business as customers pay their bills, but until that happens you'll have a cash deficiency. For at least the first month (and probably most of the second), you'll need an extra $5,000 or $6,000 in monthly working capital to support the increase.

Without an outside source to draw on, where will you get the cash? Much of the time, the first thing a business owner does is to tap the dollars normally used to pay overhead, but the firm quickly finds that the phone company doesn't like to wait for its cash any more than the firm does. Therefore the owner often turns to the one area where cash can be removed without hearing a bunch of complaints: inventory. That's an easy source of funds and the cash not used to replenish inventory doesn't affect the inventory until a few months have gone by. Then sales start to drop because the company doesn't have the right number of products available for sale.

Supporting Your Sales

The best thing about the relationship between working capital and sales is that a little bit of cash can support a sales total much higher than what you start with. For Skyline Nursery, at least in its first year of business, each $1 of working capital, once it was marked up, supported $10 in sales. This means if Val can somehow add, say, another $10,000 to the working capital of her business, the company can increase its sales by ten times that amount: $100,000. With Val's figures, this is easy to calculate: $10,000 in new working capital divided by .70 (to mark it up) equals $14,286. Multiply this figure by Val's turn rate of seven, and the result, $100,000, is the sales the new working capital can support.

As you can see, it's important that businesses keep some of the dollars they make as profit. Those funds add to the working capital of the company, which means it can make more sales and thus more profit, which creates more working capital. It all snowballs.

To summarize, each dollar you add to your working capital allows an increase in sales of that dollar *plus* your markup *multiplied by* the number of times you turn that dollar into a sale over a year. The total sales each dollar of working capital can support increase geometrically.

Just because you add to your working capital doesn't automatically mean you'll sell more, of course, but at least it gives you the opportunity to do so.

```
!----------------------------------------------------------------!
!        The figures in the grid below reflect the amount of sales !
!        a one dollar increase in working capital will support     !
!        under the conditions listed (a 30% markup and a turn rate !
!        of seven times per year).                                 !
!                                                                  !
!----------------------------------------------------------------!
!        Present working capital: $50,000                         !
!        Current markup: 30%                                      !
!        Current working capital / sales turn rate: 7 times per year !
!        Current 'supportable' sales: $500,000                    !
!                                                                  !
!                 <-- Change in markup percentage ->              !
!                                                                  !
!        -2.00% -1.00%  0.00%  1.00%  2.00%  3.00%  4.00%  5.00%! !
!        --------------------------------------------------------- !
!           0   9.72   9.86  10.00  10.14  10.29  10.45  10.61  10.77 !
!           1  11.11  11.27  11.43  11.59  11.76  11.94  12.12  12.31 !
!           2  12.50  12.68  12.86  13.04  13.24  13.43  13.64  13.85 !
!Change     3  13.89  14.08  14.29  14.49  14.71  14.93  15.15  15.38 !
!in         4  15.28  15.49  15.71  15.94  16.18  16.42  16.67  16.92 !
!working    5  16.67  16.90  17.14  17.39  17.65  17.91  18.18  18.46 !
!capital    6  18.06  18.31  18.57  18.84  19.12  19.40  19.70  20.00 !
!ratio      7  19.44  19.72  20.00  20.29  20.59  20.90  21.21  21.54 !
!           8  20.83  21.13  21.43  21.74  22.06  22.39  22.73  23.08 !
!           9  22.22  22.54  22.86  23.19  23.53  23.88  24.24  24.62 !
!          10  23.61  23.94  24.29  24.64  25.00  25.37  25.76  26.15 !
!                                                                  !
!----------------------------------------------------------------!
```

Figure 3–4 Supportable sales worksheet.

Figure 3–4 is a worksheet grid Skyline Nursery created to help understand the relationship between markup, the number of times working capital turns in a year, and the effect on sales if the company increases its working capital base.

The figures inside the grid show the increase in sales each dollar of extra working capital can support using varying markups and working capital turnover rates.

Val started with the business's current figures: a working capital of $50,000 and a 30% markup. The company is currently turning its working capital (after it's been marked up) seven times per year.

For the sake of illustration, Val put some zeroes on the worksheet. It's always a good idea to have a 0,0 point, indicating no change, to check your calculations.

Figure 3–4 shows that if the firm maintains its current markup and turnover rate, it can expect a $1 increase in working capital to produce another $10 in sales. That's the figure shown at the intersection of the two zero changes. To confirm this, start with the extra $1 in working capital and mark it up 30%: $1.00/.70 = $1.43. Next, multiply this retail amount by the turnover rate of seven: $1.43 × 7 = $10. Likewise if Val increases her markup by another 1%, the sales the extra $1 of working capital can support will rise to $10.14 (the first figure under the 1% change in sales percentage). And if

Val's markup is reduced 2%, the extra $1 in working capital can support only $9.72 in additional sales. A 1% reduction allows $9.86 in sales, and so on.

One way to increase the sales your working capital can support is to increase your working capital turnover rate. Let's say Val isn't able to change the markup. If she can change her turnover rate from seven to eight times a year, each extra $1 in working capital can support $11.43 in sales.

You can change how fast your working capital turns by reducing your collection period (by instituting better collection procedures or searching for faster-paying customers). Maybe you can ask for a down payment with each job you sell. Or perhaps you should finance all installment contracts through an outside agency, rather than carrying them yourself.

Val's worksheet is compact, but you can extend it in either direction as far as you find helpful. You can also graph your own turnover rate and compare it with both your historical average and the average of the industry you're in.

Tips and Guidelines

Most business owners don't consider the long-range implications of any debt they take on when they're making a purchase. The next time your business needs a major piece of equipment, consider not only what the monthly investment will be but also what the total cost will be over the payment period.

You can reduce the total cost by financing for a shorter period of time and paying less interest. It might surprise you that the monthly payment won't be much more if you finance a new truck, for example, for two and instead of three years, but the total interest saved will be substantial. Always consider how depreciation affects your net cash position when you're thinking about making a major purchase. Play with the figures a bit to find the best payment schedule/ depreciation period for your own cash position.

Also consider what other costs—additional insurance, utility costs, and maintenance, for example—are associated with the investment. A new truck, especially one that's financed, will have a much higher insurance cost as well as higher license fees than an older vehicle.

Ask your accountant whether you should lease rather than buy a major piece of equipment. The answer depends on your tax and cash situation.

When you estimate your total costs for any new major purchase, also consider how and when that investment will influence your cash flow. Know your break-even point in advance.

Along with knowing where your funds come from, where they're spent, and how they compare with your debt, it's also important to have a long-range feel for the funds performance of your business. If it's creating enough dollars for your normal costs plus any expansion you need, then you're doing an effective job. If your business is constantly borrowing money, then it isn't generating as much cash as it should be.

To calculate how well your company is doing at creating funds, divide the sum of a number of years' worth of sources of funds from your business operations by the same number of years' total of capital expenses, inventory additions, and any cash dividends you've declared. This is called the *funds-flow adequacy ratio.* You need to use at least three years' worth of information for this ratio to be valid—most people recommend five years of data—or there will be too many fluctuations in the information.

When this ratio falls below 1:1, it means that the dollars generated internally aren't sufficient to handle the dividends the business declares and to maintain the level of growth the company has been recording.

4

Using Business Ratios to Predict Your Future

Rob, the owner of the Tire Center, found out a bit about ratios the last time his company needed a short-term loan. The Tire Center has been in business for several years, and while it specializes in selling new and used tires, the company is similar to most other small businesses: Payroll must be met every week, inventory problems have to be controlled, many large commercial accounts are allowed to charge their purchases (which means accounts receivable have to be monitored), and so on. Rob's got two office workers, six mechanics, and two college students who do much of the dirty work. Both Rob and his wife work in the business, and they're both paid a healthy salary.

One of the things the bank examined when the Tire Center applied for a loan was the compensation the company paid its officers as a percentage of total sales. Using the *Annual Statement Studies*, Rob's banker found that most retail tire stores pay their officers compensation averaging about 4% of sales. That meant (to the banker) that Rob's business, which does a total sales volume of about $700,000 a year, should pay its officers about $28,000 a year. However, the Tire Center actually recorded officers' compensation of some $50,000 a year, or about 7% of total sales.

That was enough to make the banker sit up and take notice. Fortunately, he asked Rob about it, and once Rob explained that he and his wife were both officers, there was no problem. But often when a banker sees something out of the ordinary, the loan simply gets turned down.

Your Current Ratio

This experience made Rob wonder about how his company was doing according to other ratios that businesses normally use to measure their performance. The one you might hear about the most is called the *current ratio*, which represents the relationship between your current assets and your current liabilities. As discussed earlier, *current assets* are cash or things that you expect to convert into cash during one *operating cycle* or within one year; you learned how to calculate your own operating cycle in Chapter 2. *Current liabilities* are the bills you've got to pay within the same period. They include your trade accounts, any notes that will come due during the year, any taxes due and payable, and the current portion of your long-term debt. They're considered current because you'll liquidate them from the funds you receive from current assets; thus the relationship between the two amounts.

The more you have in current assets, the easier it will be to pay your current debts. From a banking viewpoint, the higher the current ratio the better, as that gives the banker a real cushion for any loan provided to your business.

The general rule of thumb says you should have twice as much money in current assets as you have in current liabilities. Short-term lenders use this guideline to measure the health of your company, as they expect to be paid from the dollars you generate from current operations. In most cases, the higher the safety margin, the higher the current ratio is, and, as already mentioned, the safer any creditor feels about loaning you money.

While you must give your creditors a feeling of security, you don't want to have too high a current ratio, especially if it's caused by slow-paying customers or nonmoving inventory. For example, at the end of a year, you might have $60,000 in accounts receivable plus $40,000 in other current assets—a total of $100,000 in current assets. At the same time, you might have a total of $50,000 in current liabilities. That gives you a current ratio of 2:1.

Let's say your collections really slow down at the end of the next period; your accounts receivable total $80,000, while other current assets come to $40,000—a total of $120,000 in current assets.

If your liabilities were still $50,000, you'd have a 2.4:1 current ratio. In this instance, a higher ratio is not better, as it simply means you've got a lot of customers who aren't paying their bills.

Furthermore, the 2:1 figure most people consider to be the correct current ratio isn't right for all companies in all industries. If you have a large part of your current assets tied up in inventory, the 2:1 figure just doesn't apply to you. While some businesses are able to move their inventory almost daily, others cannot. The Tire Center, for example, must have a wide range of tires and other auto parts on hand at all times, which means a large percentage of its inventory will rarely move. One of the best ways to keep tabs on your own current ratio is to keep a running worksheet that details it every month.

Figure 4–1 shows this information for the Tire Center. The variance line on the bottom of the worksheet outlines all changes from the norm. For example, Rob's business historically operates with a 1.7:1 current ratio. For the month shown, the ratio is slightly higher, at 2:1.

```
: -----------------------------------------------------------------:
:                                                                  :
:                 Current ratio worksheet for June                :
:                                                                  :
:   Current assets:                                                :
:                                                                  :
:      Cash                            $ 11,000                    :
:      Accounts receivable               42,000                    :
:      Inventory                         27,000                    :
:      [_____]           [_____]                  :
:      [_____]           [_____]                  :
:                                                                  :
:      Total current assets           $ 80,000                     :
:                                                                  :
:   Current liabilities:                                           :
:                                                                  :
:      Accounts payable               $ 27,000                     :
:      Notes payable                     5,000                     :
:      Current maturities,                                         :
:        long-term debt                  8,000                     :
:      [_____]           [_____]                  :
:      [_____]           [_____]                  :
:                                                                  :
:      Total current liabilities      $ 40,000                     :
:                                                                  :
: -----------------------------------------------------------------:
:                                                                  :
:   Current ratio this period........ 2-1                          :
:   Normal current ratio............. 1.7 -1                       :
:                                                                  :
:                    Variance                       .3             :
:                                                                  :
: -----------------------------------------------------------------:
```

Figure 4–1 Current ratio worksheet for June.

```
:------------------------------------------------------------:
:                                                            :
:                 Current ratio worksheet                    :
:                                                            :
:     January.............. 1.8        Variance     .1       :
:     February............. 1.7                      Ø       :
:     March................ 1.7                      Ø       :
:     April................ 2.Ø                     .3       :
:     May.................. 2.1                     .4       :
:     June................. 2.Ø                     .3       :
:     July................. 2.2                     .5       :
:     August............... 2.4                     .7       :
:     September............ 2.3                     .6       :
:     October..............[_____]                           :
:     November.............[_____]                           :
:     December.............[_____]                           :
:                                                            :
:------------------------------------------------------------:
```

Figure 4-2   Current ratio worksheet, showing variances.

After information is calculated on the worksheet shown in Figure 4-1, it's transferred to Figure 4-2, a monthly running worksheet for Rob's current ratio. It details the first nine months of the year. There's always a slight variation from the norm (if there were no deviation, it would be cause for alarm). In Rob's case, only two months—February and March—had a current ratio that matched the business's historical average. The rest of the months all were a bit higher than normal.

Since it almost always helps to see a picture of the data, Rob charts his current ratio information and puts it on the graph shown as Figure 4-3.

Figure 4-3 plots the data from Figure 4-2 and includes a flat line that indicates the Tire Center's average current ratio. That average line, as noted on the graph, is marked with plus (+) signs, while the nine months of data are marked with small boxes.

The graph presents a disturbing picture. For some reason— you can't tell why from this data—the Tire Center's current ratio is on the rise and has been since March. Why is the business suddenly running at a higher current ratio rate? Since the current ratio compares current assets with current liabilities, the answer must be found in those numbers. What should Rob look for?

As mentioned earlier, the current ratio will rise if current assets increase while current liabilities do not. If the Tire Center is experiencing its rise because it has more cash on hand, that's probably a good thing (unless that cash would be put to better use in inventory). But it's unlikely that a jump in the current ratio will come

Current Ratio

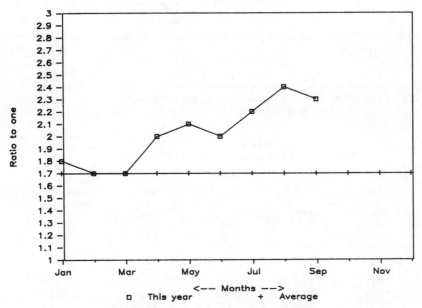

Figure 4-3 Current ratio line graph.

about for this reason; most small businesses have enough of a problem just collecting enough dollars, much less hoarding them.

The current ratio can also rise if current liabilities decrease. However, the usual way for liabilities to fall is for the business to pay them off, which causes a corresponding drop in the company's cash position—one offsets the other. Current liabilities can also decrease if some of them have been converted to long-term liabilities. But if that were the case for the Tire Center, Rob would know about it. Also, if the company had stopped paying its bills for a time, the current ratio would still remain about the same, because the cash that would have gone to pay the bills would still be in the business, and one figure would offset the other.

We can rule out a change in cash or a drop in liabilities as the reason for the Tire Center's increased current ratio. More likely, the business is experiencing a gain in either its accounts receivable or its inventory—cash is ending up stuck in one place or the other—and that's where Rob starts his examination. If it turns out that both of these areas are stable, he'll have to take a close look at the company's cash position and at its payables and other current liabilities.

Figure 4–4 details the Tire Center's inventory and accounts receivable over the past two years and nine months. It's important to look at this data on a percentage basis, rather than just the raw dollar amounts, because percentage figures give you an exact feel for your data.

```
:---------------------------------------------------------------:
:      The data is shown as a percentage                        :
:      of current assets                                        :
:                                                               :
:                                                               :
:                  Accounts                                     :
:         Cash     Receivable    Inventory                      :
:                                                               :
:   Jan     14%       52%           34%          two            :
:   Feb     15%       53%           32%          years          :
:   Mar     13%       53%           34%          ago            :
:   Apr     14%       52%           34%                         :
:   May     13%       54%           33%                         :
:   Jun     14%       52%           34%                         :
:   Jul     15%       53%           32%                         :
:   Aug     15%       53%           32%                         :
:   Sep     16%       52%           32%                         :
:   Oct     14%       54%           32%                         :
:   Nov     14%       55%           31%                         :
:   Dec     16%       51%           33%                         :
:                                                               :
:   Jan     13%       53%           34%          last           :
:   Feb     15%       53%           32%          year           :
:   Mar     14%       54%           32%                         :
:   Apr     15%       52%           33%                         :
:   May     13%       55%           32%                         :
:   Jun     12%       52%           36%                         :
:   Jul     15%       52%           33%                         :
:   Aug     15%       53%           32%                         :
:   Sep     16%       51%           33%                         :
:   Oct     14%       54%           32%                         :
:   Nov     13%       53%           34%                         :
:   Dec     16%       51%           33%                         :
:                                                               :
:   Jan     11%       57%           32%          current        :
:   Feb     11%       56%           33%          year           :
:   Mar     11%       58%           31%                         :
:   Apr     12%       57%           31%                         :
:   May     11%       55%           34%                         :
:   Jun     12%       57%           31%                         :
:   Jul     11%       58%           31%                         :
:   Aug     10%       60%           30%                         :
:   Sep     10%       60%           30%                         :
:   Oct   [____]    [____]        [____]                        :
:   Nov   [____]    [____]        [____]                        :
:   Dec   [____]    [____]        [____]                        :
:---------------------------------------------------------------:
```

Figure 4–4   Cash/accounts receivable/inventory worksheet.

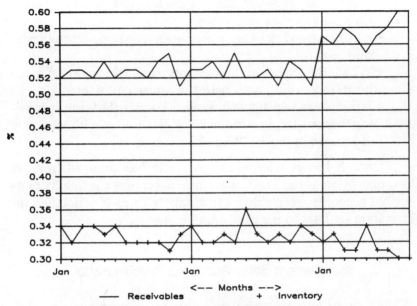

Figure 4–5 Asset percentages line graph.

As with many lists of numbers, this one is hard to understand because of the sheer amount of information it presents. You can tell that Rob's cash, as a percentage of the total, has been declining over the past nine months, and if you look closely enough, you can tell why his current ratio has been rising. But a faster, more effective way to examine this data would be to create a chart that shows both accounts receivable and inventory as a percentage of total current assets.

Figure 4–5 does just that. It shows that inventory, other than one jump in the middle of last year, stayed pretty well in the same range: always under 36% of current assets and usually in the 32%–34% range. This graph allows you to see the range.

Accounts receivable also remained stable until the start of the current year, when for some reason it left its historical range of between 52% and 54% for the first time and jumped above 56%. For the last several months, accounts receivable as a percentage of total current assets has remained high, and it looks like it's going even higher. *Why?* is the question the Tire Center would want to ask, as well as these associated questions:

- Are the accounts receivable growing larger, as a percentage of total current assets, because the business is charging more through accounts receivable?
- Are they growing because people aren't paying when they're supposed to?
- What's the quality of the accounts receivable amounts? Is the business working with better or worse customers?
- Is this percentage figure increasing because the business is selling to more, larger customers? Will it end up with too many of its eggs in too few baskets?

Once it knows why its current ratio has changed from its historical average, the Tire Center must determine the quality of its current accounts receivable total. Chapter 7 provides detailed information on how to examine aging accounts.

Your Current Sales/Accounts Payable Ratio

While the current ratio measures, at least to some degree, the ability of a business to pay its bills, there's another ratio that tells the business owner whether those invoices are being paid as they should be. This is known as the *current sales/accounts payable ratio,* and you compute it by dividing your cost of sales by the amount of your current accounts payable, then dividing the result by 365 (the number of days in a year). The ratio tells you your accounts payable turnover rate in days. If you normally buy on a net 30-day basis, you should end up with a figure close to 30. That means you're paying your bills as they come due.

For instance, if you had total costs of sales for the past year of $400,000 and currently have accounts payable of $40,000, you have a ratio of 10:1. When you divide that by 365 (days), you learn that you're paying your bills, on the average, every 36.5 days. That's a good figure if most of your suppliers let you purchase on a net 30-day basis, but it's way too long if they have net 10-day terms.

One weakness of this ratio is that it measures your bill-paying history at the end of the year or current period and thus doesn't take any seasonality into account. You'll get a better grasp of your current sales/accounts payable ratio if you track it monthly over a period of time, say on a year-to-date basis, as detailed in Figure 4–6.

Figure 4–6 is a worksheet that you can use every month to keep

```
:------------------------------------------------------------------:
:                                                                  :
:    Cost of sales / payables worksheet                            :
:------------------------------------------------------------------:
:                                                                  :
:    January:                                                      :
:                                                                  :
:    cost of sales year-to-date        30,000                      :
:    current payables                  30,000                      :
:                                                                  :
:       ratio to one: 1                                            :
:       # of days so far this year: 31                             :
:       average payable rate..................31 days              :
:                                                                  :
:-----------------------------------------------------------------:
:                                                                  :
:    February:                                                     :
:                                                                  :
:    cost of sales year-to-date        70,000                      :
:    current payables                  30,000                      :
:                                                                  :
:       ratio to one: 2.3                                          :
:       # of days so far this year: 59                             :
:       average payable rate..................26 days              :
:                                                                  :
:-----------------------------------------------------------------:
:                                                                  :
:    March:                                                        :
:                                                                  :
:    cost of sales year-to-date        110,000                     :
:    current payables                  30,000                      :
:                                                                  :
:       ratio to one: 3.7                                          :
:       # of days so far this year: 89                             :
:       average payable rate..................24 days              :
:                                                                  :
:-----------------------------------------------------------------:
:                                                                  :
:    April:                                                        :
:                                                                  :
:    cost of sales year-to-date        [_____]                   :
:    current payables                  [_____]                   :
:                                                                  :
:       ratio to one: [__]                                         :
:       # of days so far this year:[____]                          :
:       average payable rate..................[___] days           :
:                                                                  :
:-----------------------------------------------------------------:
```

Figure 4-6 Cost of sales/payable worksheet.

track of this ratio. It shows the information for the Tire Center for the first three months of the year.

To help account for seasonality, divide your cost of sales by the month-end accounts payable figure, then divide the result into the number of days so far during the year. Through January, you have 31 days; at the end of February, you've gone through 59, and so on.

For an even better picture of how well you're paying your bills, take the data a step further: Graph it. If you discover that your current sales/accounts payable ratio is growing longer—it's taking you more and more days to clear your accounts payable—it's a sign that either you're not collecting enough money or that you're not using what cash you have in the right way.

Two Sales/Assets Ratios

There are two useful internal ratio measurements that help you determine how well you're doing as a manager. Both relate the company's assets to its sales.

Every business has a specific asset amount that it uses to do business with. Some of the cash is put into inventory, so the company has something to sell. Other cash goes to daily and weekly operating costs—rent, telephone, and so on. Still other cash might be used as customer loans if the business lets customers charge their purchases through an accounts receivable system.

How you use your business's assets is an exact measurement of how successful you are. The first of these ratios compares your net fixed assets (*net fixed assets* means net of accumulated depreciation) with the sales you record. The second tells you how well you're using all the assets you have at your disposal by comparing them with your sales volume. You can compare these ratios with your own historical data as well as with that of others in your industry.

One of the difficulties in working with these ratios is that they're designed to be examined once a year. Why not break things down to a monthly basis, so you can get the data more frequently? To do this, divide your asset numbers, and the figures you plan to compare them with, by 12 (months). After all, unless you buy or sell a fixed asset, the dollar amount will remain pretty stable during the year (it's affected only by depreciation and by any payments you make against loans on your assets). By looking at these figures every month instead of at the end of the year, you may be able to correct a problem before it becomes a major difficulty.

Both of these ratios get worse as they get lower. As an example, suppose that you have $10,000 in net fixed assets and $100,000 in sales. That gives you a 10:1 ratio, which in effect says that you produced $10 in sales for every $1 in net fixed assets you have available. If you have $200,000 in sales and the same amount ($10,000) in fixed assets, each dollar of those assets creates $20 in sales.

On the other hand, if you produce only $50,000 in sales with the same fixed assets, each $1 of assets is creating only $5 in sales. As the ratio drops, it means the management of the business isn't doing as good a job as it should be.

The first ratio, which divides your sales total by your net fixed assets, gives you a good indication of how effectively your business uses its fixed assets—its trucks, machinery, and so on. Obviously, the more sales you can get from a specific set of fixed assets, the better job you're doing. If you're not doing as well as you have in the past, or as well as others in your industry, then you're not putting the right amount of cash into fixed assets. Perhaps you need to put more money into productive equipment and less into vehicles. Maybe you need to computerize to streamline your paper flow; even though this would require an investment in fixed assets, it might improve your bottom line. Or possibly you need more trucks and you've been spending too many dollars on office furniture.

The second ratio, which divides your sales volume by your total assets, measures how you're doing with your total assets, including cash, inventory, and so on. Again, the more productive you are, the more sales you'll record from the assets you have to use. As this ratio starts to fall, it means you're putting money into the wrong places. Perhaps you're allowing too many poor credit risks to charge what they buy from your business, and cash is getting stuck in your accounts receivable. Maybe your inventory selection isn't up to par, so things sit on your shelves longer than they should. Once you see a change in the wrong direction in this ratio, you should take a hard look at your accounts receivable and your inventory to see if the money you have invested there is moving. For more details on how to examine inventory data, see Chapter 7.

Since a company's total assets are almost always more than its net fixed assets, the sales/fixed asset ratio should be higher than the sales/total asset number.

Figure 4–7 lists a number of things for the Tire Center. Monthly sales are on the left, followed by monthly net fixed and total assets. In this case, since net fixed assets (for the first seven months) are shown as $4,500, you know that the Tire Center had total net fixed assets of $4,500 × 12, or $54,000. Total assets (for the first seven months) are shown as $8,000, and when that's multiplied by 12 (months), you know the business had total assets of $96,000.

The sales/asset ratios are in the last two columns. For the Tire Center, the ratio of sales to net fixed assets stayed around $12 for the first seven months of the year. In August the business added something

	Monthly Sales	Net Fixed Assets (monthly)	Total Assets (monthly)	Sales / Net fixed assets ratio	Sales / Total assets ratio
Jan	$55,000	$4,500	$8,000	$12.22	$6.88
Feb	$56,000	$4,500	$8,000	$12.44	$7.00
Mar	$55,000	$4,500	$8,000	$12.22	$6.88
Apr	$55,000	$4,500	$8,000	$12.22	$6.88
May	$58,000	$4,500	$8,000	$12.89	$7.25
Jun	$55,000	$4,500	$8,000	$12.22	$6.88
Jul	$56,000	$4,500	$8,000	$12.44	$7.00
Aug	$58,000	$6,000	$9,500	$9.67	$6.11
Sep	$59,000	$6,000	$9,500	$9.83	$6.21
Oct	$58,000	$6,000	$9,500	$9.67	$6.11
Nov	$59,000	$6,000	$9,500	$9.83	$6.21
Dec	$76,000	$6,000	$9,500	$12.67	$8.00

Figure 4–7　Worksheet detailing asset ratios.

to its asset base, and the ratio took a jump. (Rob bought a new recap machine, which will make his tire-recapping operation more efficient.) For several months toward the end of the year, the ratio dropped below $10; in December it finally came up slightly.

The sales/total asset picture looks much the same. It hovered at $7 for most of the year until the new machine was purchased, then fell. It, too, rose slightly in December.

These are the kind of results you would expect if you bought a new asset for your business. Naturally, you'd want your purchase to produce a return on your investment, but often there's no way to tell how quickly it might do so. In Rob's case, there was a bit of a lag until his tire-recapping machine started to create more sales for the company. When those sales rose, both ratios did, too, as the business was creating more sales volume with the same total assets.

Figure 4–8 plots the data from Figure 4–7. It's easier to see when the equipment was purchased and when it started creating more sales for the Tire Center.

Two other lines are charted on this graph—the historical averages of the Tire Center for the two ratios. By plotting these two other data sets, Rob gets a lot of information from a single picture; he can easily see where his current figures vary.

The average related to sales/fixed assets is at the $11 mark, and the ratio relating sales to total assets is slightly under the $7 figure. This illustration also shows that when the business purchased the new tire-recapping machine, both sales/asset ratios moved lower than

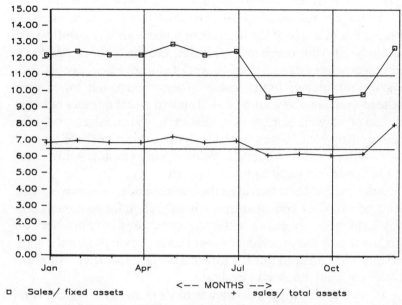

Figure 4-8 Sales compared to assets line graph.

what their average had been, then increased as the machine started to produce results. If sales hadn't increased, Rob would have had cause for concern, as that would have meant that the new purchase wasn't doing anything to help the business. It's a good sign that in December both ratio lines jumped above the company's historical average.

Often the ratios start to fall when a business spends too much in nonproductive assets. If you owned a welding business and were to buy, for instance, all new office furniture, a new copying machine, new carpeting for the office area, and other such things, you'd see your sales/fixed asset and sales/total asset ratios drop.

Other Useful Ratios

Naturally, not all ratios apply to every business, nor are they equally important to every company. The secret of ratio analysis is to find out what's meaningful for you and your people and to track only those figures.

One other ratio that's often useful compares the hours worked by your field staff with the hours put in by the people in your office. You can use the relationship between the two to manage more effectively. For example, if the number of hours your office staff works starts to bloat, your overhead total rises. On the other hand, if you can somehow get more productive work from your field people with the same number of hours in the office, then you'll lower your overhead and increase your profits. Track the total number of hours recorded by all your employees in relation to your total sales volume. By comparing your "hours worked" figure to your net profit, you'll soon discover exactly what sales volume each employee must produce for your company to make a profit.

Ask your banker what ratios the bank considers important, then learn how to collect and measure the information for your own company. You'll not only gain a better understanding of ratios but also learn how and what to present to your banker when you need a loan. Find out what form to put the information in, too; that will make it easier for your banker to evaluate.

If your business pays dividends to its shareholders from time to time, track its earnings per share. If your company doesn't provide as much growth and income as others do, your shareholders/investors will put their cash somewhere else, so this information is important to track.

Take the one ratio everyone pays attention to—profits compared with total sales—and track it on a line graph on a monthly basis. That makes it easy to spot a trend, whether upward or downward.

Look for other, less common ways to use ratio analysis. For instance, you might want to keep a running record comparing the brands of equipment you sell. Which brand is selling the most? In what area are you the most profitable? Can you expand that area? Likewise, you might want to compare a specific type of work you do with other types of work. In a construction firm, for example, you might want to compare new home sales with remodeling jobs. Where do most of your sales dollars come from? Take this broad scope and narrow it down to your employees' performance: Which service technician or installation crew do you make the most money on? A simple worksheet will let you track each worker's contribution to your company.

Comparing your current liabilities with your net worth— comparing what you owe with what you own—is a good way to evaluate your financial condition. This ratio focuses on short-term debt (your current liabilities), and as it gets higher, it tells you that you're becoming more and more dependent on your creditors.

Take it a step further and compare your total liabilities with your net worth. If this ratio gets higher than 100%, it means that your creditors have a greater equity in your company than you do. That makes it next to impossible to borrow any more funds. After all, would you loan money to a business where outsiders owned more of the company than the owner?

5

How Proper Planning Can Cut Your Costs

Modern Decorating & Design is a small business that specializes in doing just what its name says for relatively expensive homes. Owner Suzi and her staff work with a number of fine furniture stores, so they get a small percentage of the sales these stores make to Suzi's clients. Suzi also has a small shop with a number of specialty items—lamps, rugs, special glassware, china, window shades, and so on. A great deal of Suzi's direct costs are for labor, as she and her people bill for the consulting they do at an hourly rate. It's a good arrangement, since Suzi and her fellow consultants get paid even if the client doesn't buy anything.

Suzi decided to calculate all of her direct labor costs. Here's what a cost list for one of her employees looks like:

Basic hourly pay	$12.00
FICA (7.51%)	.90
Workman's compensation	.93
Federal unemployment	.09
State unemployment	.03
Vacation pay (2 weeks/year)	.48
Sick leave	.15
Net	$14.58

Suzi's business works with an overhead of 22%, which must be added to its labor cost to get a true cost picture. Since things are always figured on a retail basis, Suzi adds her overhead the same way she marks up the products she sells. To do this for any business, you first subtract your overhead percentage from the whole-number 1.

With a 22% overhead, here are the calculations: $1.00 - .22 = .78$. The labor cost is then divided by this figure (.78). Thus, Suzi divides her employee's hourly cost of $14.58 by .78, giving her a total hourly cost of $18.95. If Modern Decorating's overhead remains stable at 22%, and the cost for the employee listed doesn't increase, anything above $18.95 per hour will be profit for the business.

How to Mark Up an Item Correctly

The markup you use to determine what you charge for material (or labor) is always related to the retail price of the item. For instance, if you want to add a 20% markup to something, you don't just add a fifth of what the item costs and figure that's the correct selling price. Instead, you subtract .20 from 1.00 (which leaves .80) and then divide your cost by .80.

Here's an example. Let's say you buy something for $1. If you want to mark it up 20% and you add 20 cents, you'd have a retail price of $1.20. But when you mark something up, you want the selling price, not the cost price, to reflect your markup. You should be able to remove the markup from your retail price and end up with your actual cost. In this case, you'd want to remove the overhead amount. For these figures, you should be able to deduct 20% from the selling price of $1.20 and end up at your starting cost. If you do, however, you take 24 cents off the selling price (.24 is 20% of $1.20), which means your cost should be .96—and, of course, it isn't. That's why you need to divide the cost of your products by 1 minus your markup.

In this case, you can make sure your numbers are correct by calculating 20% of the $1.25 selling price: $1.25 \times .20 = .25$. When you subtract the .25 from $1.25, you're back at the $1 cost of the item.

Calculating Your Inventory Costs

Inventory is certainly a direct cost, as is the freight incurred to get the products to your store. And what about warehousing costs? Insurance? Is there a cost associated with keeping something in stock over a period of time? You've got to take care of it, perhaps move it from one place to another, and maybe your merchandise will lose some value as it ages. One way to calculate your exact inventory cost, without going into great detail for each individual item, is to make a list:

Total invoiced cost of items in stock	$18,000
Freight	1,100
Insurance	250
Storage cost (inventory's share of total rent)	4,800
Total inventory investment	$24,150

Your accountant can tell you exactly which costs are direct and which are not. If you look at your income statement, you'll find freight listed as a direct cost, but rarely will you see the part of your insurance that covers your inventory shown as a direct cost, and you usually won't see the part of the rent that goes for storing your inventory listed as a direct cost either. But in effect, if you didn't have any stock on hand, you wouldn't have those costs, would you? You wouldn't be paying insurance on a nonexistent inventory, nor would you need as large a building. So these items are direct costs and should be listed as such.

Decreasing Your Rent Costs

These days many businesses, particularly those in the construction trade, are able to operate with minimal facilities. When they need parts and supplies, they pick them up from a local wholesaler. What's not used for a job is returned to that supplier. The construction firm sometimes has to pay a restocking charge when things are returned, but it totals much less than renting a building. Can you change your operation so you need less space? If you're in retail sales, you obviously need a showroom, warehouse, and so on, but if you don't retail to the public, perhaps you'd be better off without a large storage area; you could use what you're now spending on rent for more productive things.

Decreasing Your Accounts Receivable Costs

There's also a cost associated with the accounts receivable your business carries, a hidden cost that many business owners often aren't aware of. If you find your company is borrowing money, then you should wonder if some of what you borrow isn't being used to maintain your accounts receivable. As an example, consider that Modern Decorating usually has about $10,000 in accounts receivable and that the business keeps an open line of credit, of which some $2,000 is used every few months for operating expenses. It gets paid back as the business collects its receivables, but at one time or another during the year, Modern Decorating is a little short of cash.

If Modern Decorating's accounts receivable total was paid as the work was completed, would the business need to borrow the $2,000 or so it needs every now and then? Assuming the company is at least breaking even, it wouldn't need the loan, so the cost of borrowing that money is an expense directly related to the fact that Modern Decorating & Design lets its customers charge their purchases.

If your own business carries accounts receivable and you need short-term cash every once in a while, consider whether you could save the cost of borrowing simply by not allowing your customers to charge what they buy from you.

Controlling Your Direct Labor and Material Costs

The way to start controlling costs, then, is to know both your direct labor and your direct material costs. Once you know them, you can track and compare them over a period of time. A quick way to do this is with a worksheet like the one shown in Figure 5–1.

Figure 5–1 is a monthly worksheet listing direct labor and direct material costs, not including overhead, for Modern Decorating. It shows the company's historical average and its total direct costs and calculates what they are as a percentage of sales. Suzi can use data from the *Annual Statement Studies* to compare her business with other businesses in the same industry. While the *Studies* doesn't list direct costs as a percentage of sales, you can use its figures to calculate what other companies average. For example, you might find these figures listed in the *Annual Statement Studies* (all are in percentages):

Net sales	100.0
Gross profit	26.0

By subtracting 26% from 100%, you can tell the business had an average direct cost total of 74%. That's what its labor and its

```
:------------------------------------------------------------------:
:                   Direct cost worksheet                          :
:                                                                  :
:                                                                  :
: January:                                                         :
:                    Sales    Direct Labor    Materials            :
: amount ->          56,000         17,000       19,000            :
: % of sales ->        100%          30.5%        33.9%            :
:                                                                  :
:       Total direct costs  64.4%  Variance this month:            :
:       Historical average  62.0%         2.4%                     :
:       Industry average    60.0%         4.4%                     :
:                                                                  :
:==================================================================:
:                                                                  :
: February:                                                        :
:                    Sales    Direct Labor    Materials            :
: amount ->          65,000         19,000       21,000            :
: % of sales ->        100%          29.2%        32.3%            :
:                                                                  :
:       Total direct costs  61.5%  Variance this month:            :
:       Historical average  62.0%        -0.5%                     :
:       Industry average    60.0%         1.5%                     :
:                                                                  :
:==================================================================:
:                                                                  :
: March:                                                           :
:                    Sales    Direct Labor    Materials            :
: amount ->          60,000         18,000       20,000            :
: % of sales ->        100%          30.0%        33.3%            :
:                                                                  :
:       Total direct costs  63.3%  Variance this month:            :
:       Historical average  62.0%         1.3%                     :
:       Industry average    60.0%         3.3%                     :
:                                                                  :
:==================================================================:
:                                                                  :
: April:                                                           :
:                    Sales    Direct Labor    Materials            :
: amount ->       [_____]      [_____]    [_____]            :
: % of sales ->   [_____]      [_____]    [_____]            :
:                                                                  :
:       Total direct costs [_____] Variance this month:            :
:       Historical average  62.0%        [_____]                   :
:       Industry average    60.0%        [_____]                   :
:                                                                  :
:==================================================================:
```

Figure 5-1   Direct cost worksheet.

associated costs (FICA, vacation pay, and so on), along with its
material and its associated costs (like freight), came to.

You can instantly see any deviation both from your historical
norm and from industry averages. As this data continues to accumulate, it's easier to see in the form of a picture, and there are
two useful graphs that you can create. The first plots the relation-

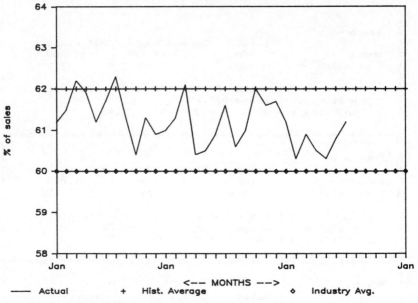

Figure 5–2   Direct cost percentages line graph.

ship between your direct cost percentage and your historical average and that of the industry you work in. For this illustration, let's use the data from Figure 5–1, which shows that Suzi's direct costs usually total 62% of her sales, while the industry averages 60%.

Figure 5–2 plots three things. The first is the historical average for Suzi's direct cost percentage and is the flat line running across at the 62% mark. The second is the flat line that represents the industry's average and runs across at 60%. The third, the line that varies, is the last 30 months of Suzi's own direct cost percentage.

According to the graph, Suzi's business is doing a good job. Her direct costs are staying right in the same range (within the same 2% spread) and appear to have her historical average as their high point and the industry's average as their low. The actual data has crossed the other lines only a couple of times. Suzi would like to reduce her direct costs—and this chart doesn't indicate that she's doing so— but at least they're not getting worse as a percentage of sales.

Figure 5–3 plots the two variance data lines in Figure 5–1. One represents the amount Modern Decorating & Design varied from its own historical average, and the other shows how the business dif-

Direct Cost Percentages

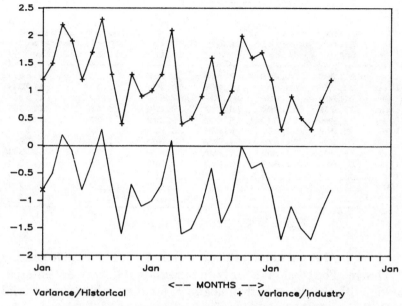

Figure 5-3   Direct cost percentages line graph.

fers from the industry average. This graph gives Suzi a different look at her numbers, as now she's charting only the differences, rather than the raw data itself. While Suzi might be upset that her costs average slightly higher than the industry average, she should take comfort in the fact that they have been averaging less than her own historical average. That in turn will, over time, lower her own average percentage figure. It means her business is moving in the right direction and that it is lowering its costs. This image makes such a change easy to see and understand.

Comparing Costs with Total Sales

You can take this data a step further by comparing both your direct labor costs and direct material costs with your total sales, but from the opposite direction. Instead of comparing each figure with total sales as a percentage of those sales, why not calculate how much in sales each produces? Businesses do this all the time with their sales-people: Joe produced X amount of sales, while JoAnn brought in Y.

```
!-----------------------------------------------------------------!
:                                                                 :
:            Direct cost data sheet                               :
:                                                                 :
:                                                                 :
:                                                                 :
:       Monthly  Monthly                    Sales per  Sales per  :
:        Labor   Material   Labor  Material   Labor    Material   :
:        Sales    Sales     Costs   Costs    Dollar    Dollar     :
:-----------------------------------------------------------------:
:Jan    21,000   56,000   17,000   36,000     1.24       1.56  :
:Feb    22,000   58,000   19,000   40,000     1.16       1.45  :
:Mar    21,000   56,000   18,000   37,000     1.17       1.51  :
:Apr    23,000   58,000   18,000   38,000     1.28       1.53  :
:May    24,000   54,000   18,000   40,000     1.33       1.35  :
:Jun    25,000   52,000   19,000   38,000     1.32       1.37  :
:Jul    23,000   50,000   18,000   38,000     1.28       1.32  :
:Aug    24,000   50,000   19,000   37,000     1.26       1.35  :
:Sep    23,000   52,000   18,000   39,000     1.28       1.33  :
:Oct [_____] [_____] [_____] [_____]    [___]      [___]  :
:Nov [_____] [_____] [_____] [_____]    [___]      [___]  :
:Dec [_____] [_____] [_____] [_____]    [___]      [___]  :
!-----------------------------------------------------------------!
```

Figure 5–4   Direct cost data sheet.

Figure 5–4 is a more detailed worksheet for Modern Decorating & Design. The total sales for both materials and labor are entered, along with the direct cost breakdown for the company's material and labor costs. Monthly sales for labor are divided by direct labor, and monthly sales for materials are divided by direct material costs and listed in the last two columns of this worksheet.

If you calculate the percentages, you'll find that direct labor runs about 25% of total sales, while materials make up about 50% of total sales. Total costs averaged 75% of each sales dollar. That gives this business about 25% to work with in terms of overhead costs and profit.

Each sales and costs figure in Figure 5–4 varies slightly. In January, for example, labor recorded $1.24 in sales volume for each $1 in labor costs. In February that figure fell to $1.16, in March it was $1.17, and so on. January's material costs recorded sales of $1.56 per cost dollar, February's were $1.45, and so on. Just looking at the numbers, it's difficult for Suzi to get a line on what's happening, but when she charts the information, she can see that her business has a problem with its material sales.

Figure 5–5 plots the last two columns in Figure 5–4, where the sales dollar per each cost amount are listed. During the first part of this year, materials produced considerably more in sales volume, per dollar spent, than labor did. There was roughly a 30-cent difference for each of the first three months. Something happened in May, when all of a sudden Suzi's material sales and labor sales for

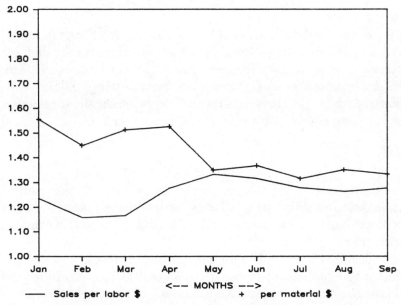

Figure 5–5   Sales per direct cost dollar line graph.

each cost dollar were about the same. They've remained steady from May through September.

What causes this kind of change? It's easy to tell from the picture that while labor's sales rose slightly, material sales have fallen. Only three reasons can account for such a drop. One is that material costs have increased without a corresponding rise in the selling price of the products. The second possibility is that Suzi purchased materials that have not been moving but instead are sitting in inventory. The third reason is that material costs have remained stable, but the retail selling price has decreased. Let's take a closer look at these reasons.

Suzi needs to go back over her records for this period and examine both her material costs and her markup percentage. If her material costs have increased, she must figure out why. If inventory has risen during this period, Suzi knows that's where the problem is and can correct it. Perhaps she needs to be more careful making purchases or must spend more time marketing the products.

She may also discover that costs for her goods have increased, but for some reason, the retail selling prices don't reflect the new, higher costs. Was the business overcharged for the products it bought?

Is it now paying for freight, where before purchases came prepaid? These, too, are easy things to check: Just look back at the last few months' bills.

If Suzi finds that she's not buying and storing things in her inventory, and that her material costs have remained stable, then her markup has gone down for some reason. It may be because of increased competition, special sales promotions, or sloppy billings (some materials didn't get charged to the right invoices). Again, it's a matter of checking costs against how things were charged.

Lowering Your Overhead

In addition to its direct cost totals for labor and materials, every business has overhead to contend with, and it's usually a constant struggle to try to lower it.

Overhead, also called an indirect cost, are those expenses you must pay whether or not you make any sales. These include your salary, the rent, your electric bill, and so on. In other words, these are the dollars it takes to keep your doors open.

Business owners have been taught to examine their overhead by calculating it as a percentage of sales. If your overhead totals $60,000 and you have total sales of $300,000, you divide $60,000 by $300,000, which gives you an overhead percentage of 20%.

It's also worthwhile to track your overhead information over time and compare it with your historical average and with that of other businesses in your industry. If you discover you're out of line in either case, it's cause for concern and will alert you to examine your overhead in detail.

Figure 5–6 is a worksheet that Modern Decorating & Design uses to keep track of its overhead. It's shown both as a dollar value and as a percentage of total sales. The company's historical average is listed, as is the industry average. Variations also are shown.

Figure 5–7 plots three lines for overhead as a percentage of sales. The flat line that runs across at 21% charts the historical average for Modern Decorating. The other flat line plots the industry average and runs across at 22%. The line that varies charts the business's overhead percentage during the past 18 months.

Suzi should be pleased with this picture, as the overhead as a percentage of sales for her business has been consistently under both her historical average and that of the industry she works in. Her

```
---------------------------------------------------------------
:                                                             :
:                   Overhead worksheet                        :
:                                                             :
:   January:                                                  :
:                    Sales      Overhead                      :
:   amount ->        56,000      12,000                        :
:   % of sales ->     100%       21.4%                         :
:                                                             :
:       Historical average  21.0%   Variance:  0.4%           :
:       Industry Average    22.0%   Variance: -0.6%           :
:       Reverse overhead amount: $ 4.66                        :
:                                                             :
:=============================================================:
:   February:                                                 :
:                    Sales      Overhead                      :
:   amount ->        65,000      13,000                        :
:   % of sales ->     100%       20.0%                         :
:                                                             :
:       Historical average  21.0%   Variance: -1.0%           :
:       Industry average    22.0%   Variance: -2.0%           :
:       Reverse overhead amount: $ 5.00                        :
:                                                             :
:=============================================================:
:   March:                                                    :
:                    Sales      Overhead                      :
:   amount ->        60,000      13,000                        :
:   % of sales ->     100%       21.6%                         :
:                                                             :
:       Historical average  21.0%   Variance:  0.6%           :
:       Industry Average    22.0%   Variance: -0.4%           :
:       Reverse overhead amount: $ 4.61                        :
:                                                             :
:=============================================================:
:   April:                                                    :
:                    Sales      Overhead                      :
:   amount ->        [_____]    [_____]                     :
:   % of sales ->     100%       [_____]                     :
:                                                             :
:       Historical average  21.0%   Variance: [_____]         :
:       Industry average    22.0%   Variance: [_____]         :
:       Reverse overhead amount: [_____]                      :
:                                                             :
:=============================================================:
```

Figure 5-6 Overhead worksheet.

overhead is decreasing—exactly what any business owner would want to happen.

You can take this further by plotting the variances from the norm, rather than the raw data. To do so, you'd plot two variance lines: one that shows the deviation from your historical average and one that shows how your percentage differs from the industry average. Your graph would be similar to the one in Figure 5-3. In Suzi's case,

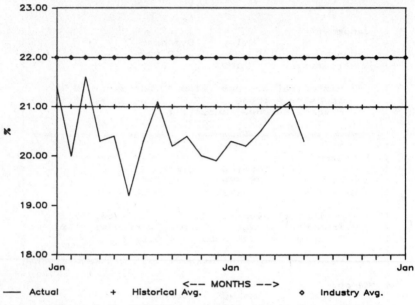

Figure 5–7   Overhead percentage of sales line graph.

because her average is lower than both her historical average and the industry average, both plotted lines will be lower than the zero mark. This would confirm what you see in Figure 5–7: Suzi's doing a good job at reducing her overhead as a percentage of sales.

Your Reverse Overhead Figure

Do you get the feeling that the more you cut costs and lower your overhead, the more difficult it is to stay in the black? That's because there's something of a paradox in business that involves both your sales and your overhead totals.

The last line of each entry in Figure 5–6 shows what I call the *reverse,* or *backward overhead figure.* Why not try to look at your overhead from a different direction to gain another perspective? Instead of dividing your overhead by your sales, divide your total sales by your overhead. Using the numbers from the example earlier, you would divide $300,000 in sales by $60,000 in overhead for a result of $5. This is the dollar volume of sales you have to make to pay for a $1 increase in your overhead total if you want to keep your overhead as a percentage of sales at its current level.

If you want to give the two people on your office staff (whose salary is included in your total overhead) each a raise of $2,000 per year, you'd have to increase sales by $20,000 just to break even. This is because your business now has a 5:1 ratio: An overhead of 20% means the overhead dollars will divide into the sales total five times. Again, to keep its overhead at the current percentage level, your company must sell $5 for every $1 it adds to its overhead total.

If you want to buy, say, a new telephone system, and this year's share of the payments will run $3,000, you'll have to sell five times that amount—$15,000—just to pay for the purchase.

Suppose you really work at reducing your overhead, and it drops from $60,000 to $50,000. Your overhead as a percentage of sales then goes from 20% to 17%, a drop any businessperson would be pleased with. But the backward figure moves from $5 to $6 (you divide your sales of $300,000 by your new overhead of $50,000). Now to justify a $1 increase in overhead, you have to somehow raise sales by $6.

That's where the paradox is: The more successful you are at reducing overhead, the harder it is to control your basic costs. This is something not enough business owners are aware of and can be a crucial factor in deciding whether to buy an item, approve a raise for an employee, and so on.

In Figure 5–8, the numbers running up and down the left side of the worksheet represent a range of monthly overhead amounts. The figures across the top represent a range of sales totals. The numbers inside the grid represent the backward overhead figures, calculcated by dividing the monthly sales amounts by the overhead totals.

For example, with sales of $30,000 and overhead of $8,000 a month, you would need to increase sales by $3.75 for each $1 you increased your overhead total (the $3.75 is the figure at the intersection of $30,000 in sales and overhead of $8,000).

Likewise, if you have monthly sales of $35,000 and a monthly overhead of $10,000, you'd need to increase sales by $3.50 for each extra $1 you spend on overhead. But with that same overhead and a monthly sales total of only $30,000, you have to raise sales only $3 for every extra $1 you spend on new overhead. (Of course, that also means your overhead percentage is 33.3%, which is higher than most businesses would want.)

```
!---------------------------------------------------------------!
!                   Backwards Overhead totals                   !
!                                                               !
!Overhead              <-- Monthly sales -->                    !
!totals      30,000    31,000    32,000    33,000    34,000    35,000 !
!   VV   !-------------------------------------------------------!
!   8,000 !  $3.75     $3.88     $4.00     $4.13     $4.25     $4.38 !
!   8,100 !  $3.70     $3.83     $3.95     $4.07     $4.20     $4.32 !
!   8,200 !  $3.66     $3.78     $3.90     $4.02     $4.15     $4.27 !
!   8,300 !  $3.61     $3.73     $3.86     $3.98     $4.10     $4.22 !
!   8,400 !  $3.57     $3.69     $3.81     $3.93     $4.05     $4.17 !
!   8,500 !  $3.53     $3.65     $3.76     $3.88     $4.00     $4.12 !
!   8,600 !  $3.49     $3.60     $3.72     $3.84     $3.95     $4.07 !
!   8,700 !  $3.45     $3.56     $3.68     $3.79     $3.91     $4.02 !
!   8,800 !  $3.41     $3.52     $3.64     $3.75     $3.86     $3.98 !
!   8,900 !  $3.37     $3.48     $3.60     $3.71     $3.82     $3.93 !
!   9,000 !  $3.33     $3.44     $3.56     $3.67     $3.78     $3.89 !
!   9,100 !  $3.30     $3.41     $3.52     $3.63     $3.74     $3.85 !
!   9,200 !  $3.26     $3.37     $3.48     $3.59     $3.70     $3.80 !
!   9,300 !  $3.23     $3.33     $3.44     $3.55     $3.66     $3.76 !
!   9,400 !  $3.19     $3.30     $3.40     $3.51     $3.62     $3.72 !
!   9,500 !  $3.16     $3.26     $3.37     $3.47     $3.58     $3.68 !
!   9,600 !  $3.13     $3.23     $3.33     $3.44     $3.54     $3.65 !
!   9,700 !  $3.09     $3.20     $3.30     $3.40     $3.51     $3.61 !
!   9,800 !  $3.06     $3.16     $3.27     $3.37     $3.47     $3.57 !
!   9,900 !  $3.03     $3.13     $3.23     $3.33     $3.43     $3.54 !
!  10,000 !  $3.00     $3.10     $3.20     $3.30     $3.40     $3.50 !
!---------------------------------------------------------------!
```

Figure 5-8   Backwards overhead totals.

It's important to note that this is all based on the theory that you want to keep your overhead, as a percentage of your sales, at its current level.

Tips and Guidelines

When you purchase something, consider its operating costs along with its initial price. Often with machinery, tools, and vehicles, the operating costs make up a significant percentage of the item's total cost. Also consider the maintenance costs for each piece of equipment or machinery you have as part of the expense of owning the item.

For example, you might purchase computer software that's subject to a yearly update fee (sometimes 15% of the initial purchase price). Software many companies use, like Lotus 1-2-3 or Word-Perfect, is constantly changing, which means an extra expense to purchase an updated version.

Always comparison-shop. In my business, for example, I know that one manufacturer charges less than another for its line of furnaces but more for its air-conditioning units. I get quotations on every individual job to avoid paying more than I should for equipment. This way I won't lose a job because my estimates are higher than the competition's.

Design a system that will track every invoice your company receives. This makes sure each thing you purchase is charged, at the correct price, to the right job. It's much easier to not do this, as there's a lot of paperwork involved, but it's often the only way a business can get a true handle on its costs. If you own a microcomputer, this is an ideal task for it. Simply get a program that will allow you to create a job file for each job you do and post every invoice to the proper job.

To reduce your overhead, pick a different area every month and concentrate on its costs. Learn all you can about the particular item, so you'll know exactly where each dollar goes. This is really an eye-opener, as many small business owners don't know how much they're spending on advertising, for office supplies, and so on.

Examine the time sheets your employees produce with an eye to "free" time—quarter and half hours that are charged to the business rather than to a specific job. Everyone spends time waiting on the phone, running back to the shop for a part, and so on. Go back over your employee's time cards for the past month or two and add up their productive and nonproductive time. Once you determine how much nonproductive time your people spend, figure out what percentage of your total labor costs it is. You'll be amazed—and probably saddened—by how many labor hours are not charged out.

Calculate your overhead on a daily or even an hourly basis. It's useful to know what it costs to just open your doors every morning, whether you sell anything or not. You can also get a terrific feel for where your cash has gone just by reading the data in your checkbook.

Take a look at the maintenance costs for each vehicle and compare them. What truck costs you the most, per mile, to operate? The least? This will be useful information when it comes time to trade one of them for a new vehicle.

Are there higher overhead and/or direct costs associated with a specific type of job your business does? From an ordering standpoint, it often takes just as much time and as much paperwork to order a $5 item as it does for a $5,000 product. Can you eliminate any of the sales that don't cover their own internal costs, or perhaps add a service fee to their bills, to at least cover your overhead? Break down your cost totals so they make sense for you and your company; then you'll be able to get a handle on them.

6

Life and Death with Leverage

Quality Plumbing is a small contracting business that's had a few good years and is now encountering tougher competition, a changing market that's becoming more service-oriented, and a growing community and wider customer base that will require the business to reach out further than it ever has before.

Phil, Quality Plumbing's owner, feels his trucks need upgrading, if for no other reason than good customer acceptance. He decides to buy one new and three used trucks. The monthly payment, secured by the vehicles, of course, comes to $950.

Then the big rig Phil's got on the back of the old flatbed truck—the machine that cleans out septic tanks—breaks down, and the cost to repair it seems way too high. Phil finds that the business can lease another such machine, one that's more modern and so should be more efficient, for $275 a month. Since that seems to make more sense than throwing good money after bad in repairing the old unit, that's what the company does. It also makes sense to lease rather than purchase, because—in Phil's mind—the lease won't add to what the business owes his bank. He'll still be able to turn to the bank if he needs more funds in the future.

A month later Phil spends some time with a salesperson who persuades Phil (who doesn't really take much convincing) that what Quality Plumbing needs is a two-way radio system. When all the costs are figured in, the thing should pay for itself just in the time saved in running back to the office to get the next service call. It also will allow the company a wider area to do business in, as Phil will now be able to schedule more service calls during each working day. Business is good and the radios seem a sound investment. Monthly payment: $400.

The bottom line ends up something like this: Six months ago Quality Plumbing had little long-term debt, except for its building, and now the business has monthly payments in excess of $1,600. The payments will go on for the next four years.

Sure, all the purchases make sense: The trucks and the new machine are necessities, and for Quality Plumbing to continue to grow, two-way radios in all the service trucks are a must.

But Phil has ignored some extra costs that are associated with these payments. Insurance and license fees for the new vehicles will be higher than for his old trucks, he may have to pay more taxes on the new piece of equipment, the radios will have to be installed, and so on.

Phil made still another mistake. He didn't give any thought to what the *total* payment would be for all these necessary things or to what the business can handle. Phil didn't realize that the company was now responsible for $1,625 per month in new payments . . . or $19,500 a year . . . or $78,000 over the four-year span it will take to pay all these purchases off. Often a business owner will look at all the little trees and not see enough of the big forest until he's lost in it.

Where will those dollars come from? How much more in sales volume will Quality Plumbing have to tally up just to make the payments? Will the new equipment directly add to Phil's sales total? Let's find out if Phil's company is overleveraged.

Calculating Leverage

When a company borrows money from a bank, it is using *leverage:* the idea that the profits it will make with those dollars will exceed the costs of borrowing. That's also true when a company purchases, say, a new truck for its service department; it hopes that the new vehicle will save time and the cost of repairs. Sometimes a business must use leverage—to purchase a building, for example. When a company buys parts and equipment from a wholesaler, on a net 30-day basis, it's using the supplier's money, starting from the time it picks up the materials until it sends the wholesaler a check. When it finances insurance payments over a year, whether through an insurance company, agent, or bank, it's using leverage. Customers who charge their purchases through an accounts receivable system are using the company for leverage.

A hundred years or so ago, small companies didn't use much leverage. Purchases were paid for immediately, and employees were paid every night. Other than perhaps letting customers use leverage by charging their purchases, businesses generally operated on a cash-only basis.

Things started to change when business owners discovered that more money could be made by using leverage in an intelligent way. Somewhere along the line, businesses started paying their employees every week or every two weeks, which gave the company time to come up with the cash. A smart wholesaler learned that sales would grow if customers were allowed to charge what they bought, in effect letting the business work on the supplier's money. About the only people you can't get some leverage from nowadays is the Internal Revenue Service, which insists that it get its cash on time and charges you if you take an extension.

The Pitfalls of Too Much Leverage

These days it's often too easy to become overextended; if you have a decent financial statement, most banks will lend you money for anything you want to purchase. There are still other types of leverage difficulties that are just as easy to get into, and they are hard to get out of because they're not often recognized as problems until you're deeply caught up in them. Say a company all of a sudden finds itself in a fast-growing market that requires it to purchase new trucks, machinery, and equipment and to raise more dollars just to operate—all at the same time. That's what happened to Phil's company.

Quality Plumbing has about $40,000 a month in sales, a direct cost percentage of 70%, an overhead of 25%, and a net profit before taxes of about 5%. To cover Phil's new payments of $1,625 per month, the business must either lower its overhead or increase sales. Otherwise, the dollars will come right out of profit. In Phil's case, that's not going to work, because the $1,625 payment will just about eat away his profit of $2,000 a month. Phil will have to increase sales to keep his profit at the same level.

Let's further assume that all additional sales will go toward servicing the new debt. This means that the present level of sales will still take care of the overhead burden. For every $1,000 in sales it records, Quality Plumbing has $300 in cash left over after it pays its direct costs. To come up with $1,625 every month, the business must make new sales of about $5,400 (30% of $5,400 is $1,620).

Once this figure has been determined, the business owner can figure out if the new purchases will pay for themselves. In Phil's case, he's got to consider:

Will the new trucks really increase sales? How? Like many fixed assets, new trucks change the overhead total but often don't improve sales volume unless they somehow allow employees to do more work.

While fewer and smaller repair bills on the vehicles mean lower overhead, how much money will go for insurance and taxes? Phil must factor this amount into his calculations.

How much more efficient will the new machine make the pumping crew? How can that be translated into greater sales? One extra call a day will bring in $50, which is $250 a week, or about $1,100 a month over a year. That's about 20% of the new sales Phil needs.

Will the radios add to sales? How? Will each of the three service technicians be able to get to an extra call or two every day just because the radios will make them more efficient? If each extra call brings in $30, Phil can expect $90 a day, or $450 a week, or about $2,000 a month.

If these are the best ideas Phil can come up with, he's got a problem. The new purchases will add $3,000 or perhaps a bit more to the company's sales, and that isn't enough. At a gross profit of 30%, $3,000 in sales creates only $900, or some $725 less than the new monthly payment total.

Phil needs to figure out some way to get even more use from the new equipment. Perhaps he can generate sales by promoting the new look the trucks give his business or by discovering how the radios can help his service people do more than one new call every day.

Figure 6–1 is a grid that details the payments a business can come up with at varying sales and gross profit levels. It assumes that all the gross profits that are produced from the new sales will be used to support the new payments—a situation not likely to occur in the real world. This assumption is made because it makes the example easier to see and understand. Most companies experience some in-

```
                    <-- New monthly sales -->

              $5,000    $6,000    $7,000    $8,000    $9,000    $10,000
          ---------------------------------------------------------------
       20%! $1,000    $1,200    $1,400    $1,600    $1,800    $2,000  !
       21%! $1,050    $1,260    $1,470    $1,680    $1,890    $2,100  !
       22%! $1,100    $1,320    $1,540    $1,760    $1,980    $2,200  !
       23%! $1,150    $1,380    $1,610    $1,840    $2,070    $2,300  !
gross  24%! $1,200    $1,440    $1,680    $1,920    $2,160    $2,400  !
profit 25%! $1,250    $1,500    $1,750    $2,000    $2,250    $2,500  !
percent 26%! $1,300   $1,560    $1,820    $2,080    $2,340    $2,600  !
       27%! $1,350    $1,620    $1,890    $2,160    $2,430    $2,700  !
       28%! $1,400    $1,680    $1,960    $2,240    $2,520    $2,800  !
       29%! $1,450    $1,740    $2,030    $2,320    $2,610    $2,900  !
       30%! $1,500    $1,800    $2,100    $2,400    $2,700    $3,000  !
       31%! $1,550    $1,860    $2,170    $2,480    $2,790    $3,100  !
       32%! $1,600    $1,920    $2,240    $2,560    $2,880    $3,200  !
       33%! $1,650    $1,980    $2,310    $2,640    $2,970    $3,300  !
       34%! $1,700    $2,040    $2,380    $2,720    $3,060    $3,400  !
       35%! $1,750    $2,100    $2,450    $2,800    $3,150    $3,500  !
          ---------------------------------------------------------------
```

Figure 6-1 New monthly sales worksheet.

crease in overhead along with any sales increase, so they need a greater increase in sales to be able to handle a particular payment amount.

Running up and down the left side of Figure 6-1 is a range of gross profits from 20% to 35%. Across the top of the grid are new sales figures—the amount the business will try to record to raise the extra cash it needs. The entries inside the grid multiply the gross profit percentages by the amounts along the top. For example, a 20% gross profit with a new sales total of $5,000 will produce a gross of $1,000 (the $1,000 is in the upper-left-hand corner of the worksheet at the intersection of $5,000 in sales and 20% in gross profit). If the business averages a gross profit of 25% and can create additional monthly sales of $9,000, it will create $2,250 in extra cash every month.

You might want to make a more detailed worksheet for yourself. For example, if your gross profit usually averages 23%, you might create a grid that varies in quarter-point increments, perhaps in a range from 21% to 25% (two percentage points higher and lower than your average). If the new machinery you're thinking about purchasing creates between $5,000 and $7,000 a month in extra sales, you might end up with a grid like Figure 6-2.

Figure 6-2 is designed for a specific group of numbers and details a smaller range of figures than Figure 6-1 did. Here you can see that if your new equipment will create sales of $6,000, and you average a gross profit percentage of 23%, the new sales will add $1,380 to your monthly gross. If your payments are higher than $1,380, the remainder will come out of your profits. If that's the case, you'd probably want to avoid making the purchase.

<-- New monthly sales -->

		$5,000	$5,500	$6,000	$6,500	$7,000
	21.00%	$1,050	$1,155	$1,260	$1,365	$1,470
	21.25%	$1,063	$1,169	$1,275	$1,381	$1,488
	21.50%	$1,075	$1,183	$1,290	$1,398	$1,505
	21.75%	$1,088	$1,196	$1,305	$1,414	$1,523
gross	22.00%	$1,100	$1,210	$1,320	$1,430	$1,540
profit	22.25%	$1,113	$1,224	$1,335	$1,446	$1,558
percent	22.50%	$1,125	$1,238	$1,350	$1,463	$1,575
	22.75%	$1,138	$1,251	$1,365	$1,479	$1,593
	23.00%	$1,150	$1,265	$1,380	$1,495	$1,610
	23.25%	$1,163	$1,279	$1,395	$1,511	$1,628
	23.50%	$1,175	$1,293	$1,410	$1,528	$1,645
	23.75%	$1,188	$1,306	$1,425	$1,544	$1,663
	24.00%	$1,200	$1,320	$1,440	$1,560	$1,680
	24.25%	$1,213	$1,334	$1,455	$1,576	$1,698
	24.50%	$1,225	$1,348	$1,470	$1,593	$1,715
	24.75%	$1,238	$1,361	$1,485	$1,609	$1,733
	25.00%	$1,250	$1,375	$1,500	$1,625	$1,750

Figure 6–2 New monthly sales worksheet. (Figures are more exact.)

As mentioned earlier, before you make a purchase, you should consider its total cost, rather than just the monthly payment involved. If you're thinking about, say, a new high-speed copier for your office, you would naturally consider whether your customers see the copies you make (if they don't, perhaps you don't need one that produces perfect copies), as well as how much time your office people will save with the new machine. But also keep in mind the total amount you'll spend on the copier. Financed over a three-year period, a $240 monthly payment comes to $8,640. You need to know this before you sign the papers.

Leverage Problems for the Cash Buyer

Let's also realize that leverage difficulties don't happen only to companies that spend too much on fixed assets. That's the most common problem, but it's not unusual for a growing business with no monthly payments to find itself in trouble because it overleverages itself.

This happens because of the way most companies do business: rarely all-cash, in terms of what they buy, but rather on an open-account basis with any number of suppliers. If business takes place as it should, your customers pay you for the work you do and you in turn pay your suppliers. Unfortunately, your customers might not pay as they're supposed to, and you, as the business owner/manager, might not properly distribute the dollars you do collect.

When your growing business expands, it calls more and more on its suppliers for credit, and the suppliers are eager to help, particularly if your business has been discounting its bills. Your suppliers see your company as a good credit risk: Month after month, you take their offered trade discount, so they assume your cash is flowing in just as it should, that you're making the right business decisions (one of those decisions is to pay the supplier), and so on.

There's no problem as long as the business continues to collect for its work as it finishes each job, but sooner or later some customer—often a major one—is slow paying a bill. That often results in your business not being able to pay its suppliers for at least part of what it owes.

Let's say something like this happened to Quality Plumbing right after it expanded. Phil was doing pretty well until he bid on and got a good-size job for a local contractor who was building a large office building. Because he had worked for the contractor in the past, Phil didn't ask for any special payment terms or any money as a down payment but started billing him on a monthly basis as the work was completed.

This went along fine for two months, but then one month the contractor skipped a payment. Phil did the right thing and called the contractor, but it didn't produce the results he had hoped for. The contractor told Phil that there had been a few problems with the job, and even though they weren't plumbing problems, the building owner had held back part of his monthly payment, which left the contractor short of funds. He assured Phil that all the money would be forthcoming the following month. Now Phil is providing more leverage to this one large customer than he had planned on. As a result, Phil used his own working capital to pay his employees and suppliers, but now he himself is short on cash.

The next month it happens again. Now Quality Plumbing is a little behind—nothing major, not anything to worry about, but still behind. Phil won't have the resources to pay his suppliers in full until his slow-paying customer pays him. So Phil starts to juggle his supplier accounts just a bit—paying one off and buying heavily from that one until that account ages a little, then buying from another while he works at paying off the first wholesaler.

This doesn't become a big problem unless one of two things happens. The first would be if the contractor who owes Phil a good hunk of cash goes down the drain and Phil ends up holding the bag. Or, if this large contractor does pay what he owes, and Phil has problems with one of his other large accounts, he'll find himself cash-short again, with more juggling to do. It's almost as easy to get behind with your suppliers as it is at the bank, and if you misuse your accounts payable leverage you can pay cash for all of your fixed assets and still find your business in serious trouble. Of course, someone you've bought a fixed asset from—a truck, for example—can come and take it back if you don't make the payments, but wholesalers usually don't have this option. Instead, your suppliers can sue you or lien your job or at the very least, cut off your credit. It really doesn't matter whether you're dealing with fixed assets or other purchases; if you don't pay for them, your business has problems.

Tracking the Age of Your Accounts Payable

One thing that gives you a good feel for how you're using the type of leverage that you have when you buy from a wholesaler is to track the average age of your accounts payable. By doing this on a regular basis, you can get a good idea of how your business looks to your creditors. If your business is able to clear the board every month by paying everything it owes, then you're in terrific shape and simply need to watch for any slippage—months when you aren't able to pay everything in full. Many small companies, however, let at least a few of their payables slide once in a while.

Figure 6–3 is a worksheet that makes it easy to figure out the age of an accounts payable account. All you have to do is to list each current invoice and its date, and then calculate how old that particular bill is. Then you just add the listings of the age of each current obligation and average them out. If your suppliers normally ask for payment within 30 days, you should have an average close to 30. In this illustration, the business is running about 15 days behind what its suppliers request. What kind of a credit reference would they provide?

It's very useful to keep a running record of this average, as you'll be able to see those times that your business has cash problems and those when it stays current with its bills. Usually the best way to keep such a record is with a line graph that covers a long period of time. Then you can just do your calculations each month and fill in the chart.

```
┌─────────────────────────────────────────────────────────────┐
│                                                               │
│   Accounts payable aging worksheet                            │
│                                                               │
│   Date: 11/15/99                                              │
│                                                               │
│                                                               │
│   Supplier                   Invoice date    Days old         │
│                                                               │
│   Ash Fork Wholesale          10/21/99          25            │
│   Phoenix Mercantile          09/19/99          57            │
│   Western Suppoly             10/01/99          45            │
│   Phoenix Cooling             09/15/99          53            │
│   State Insurance Fund        10/01/99          45            │
│   _____        __/__/__         ___            │
│   _____        __/__/__         ___            │
│   _____        __/__/__         ___            │
│                                              _____       │
│                                                               │
│                              total:            225            │
│                                                               │
│                                                               │
│   Total days old divided by the number of suppliers:          │
│                                                               │
│      225   /   5    =    45 days old, on average              │
│                                                               │
└─────────────────────────────────────────────────────────────┘
```

Figure 6–3   Accounts payable aging worksheet.

Figure 6–4, a line chart that details the average age of Quality Plumbing's accounts payable totals, has room for three years information. Phil started this chart by plotting a straight line for what he expected his average to be, or what his suppliers normally request. In this example, he plotted a straight line at 30 days, the time period in which he should be paying his bills. When you create your own accounts payable aging chart, you too should plot a straight line representing your normal or expected payment terms.

The other line, the one that varies, records Phil's own record. In this illustration, he's plotted nineteen months of data, and what he ends up with is not a good picture. When Phil started calculating and charting the average age of his accounts payable, he stayed within a few days of where he wanted to be. Lately, however, Phil's climbed above the 30-day-payment mark, meaning that his bills are getting slightly older. Worse yet, the trend seems to be generally upward. Why isn't Phil paying his bills as quickly as he once did?

There can be any number of reasons for a change in the way a business pays its bills. It's not likely that it's been caused by just one customer not paying what he owed Quality Plumbing, although one major customer can start a business on the road to money difficulties. If a problem persists over a period of time—as it has for

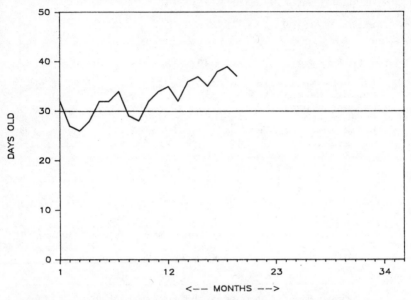

Figure 6-4   Line graph showing average age of accounts payable.

Phil—then it's more probable that it's caused by a number of people not paying their bills on time.

The easy way to check this is to make an aging worksheet for your accounts receivable accounts, just as you did for your accounts payable. That will show you which accounts are not paying when they promised they would.

Obviously, you won't be able to pay your bills until your customers pay you. If you have an average collection period of 30 days, you'll be able to pay your suppliers on a net-30 basis. How to compute your average collection period and how it affects your cash flow are discussed in Chapter 7.

Leverage and Long-Term Debts

Each business has specific obligations that limit the amount of new debt it can handle comfortably. Out of each dollar a company receives from sales, it must pay a percentage for materials, another for the labor it uses, a certain amount for overhead, and so on. Every company has a definite limit it should maintain between its debt and available working capital. This is especially true for long-term debt, those obligations a business creates when it can't afford to fund a purchase within the next year or operating cycle. Long-term obligations affect your cash position because some of your working capital is always used to pay for the debt. While you intend (and must) replace this working capital with funds generated, the fact is that— from a cash standpoint—you need to have the money available to make the required payments when they come due. Before you take out a long-term debt, you must project into the future and make an educated guess as to whether or not you'll be able to make the payments.

Once you have an accurate projection, you can then work in reverse to determine whether your existing or anticipated debt load is too great. If you know that other businesses like yours usually operate with a long-term debt to sales ratio of 10:1, and you project your sales for next year to be $500,000, you know your long-term debt load should be, at most, about $50,000. If it's lower than that, you can probably take on some more long-term debt; if it's higher, you're probably going to have difficultly repaying your loans.

Several ratios, using guidelines from the *Annual Statement Studies,* are useful. Before Phil purchased his new trucks and equipment for his company, he should have looked up some information in the *Studies* to determine his debt ratios.

For example, he might have figured out the ratios between long-term debt and working capital, available cash and short-term loans, and so on. The important thing is to make these kinds of comparisons before you buy whatever it is you're considering. Once you sign the loan papers, it's too late.

One measurement Phil would have found useful is the ratio between long-term debt and sales, which predicts whether the company will generate sufficient sales to produce enough cash to handle its debt. He might have discovered that other businesses in his industry, doing about the same sales as his company, have about a 9–1 ratio: For every $9 in sales, they have $1 in long-term debt. If Phil's own figure is lower than the industry average, he's probably able to take on more debt and vice versa.

Another measurement compares your cash flow with the current portion of your long-term debt—the part that's due this year. (Cash flow is defined here as net profit plus depreciation.) This comparison tells you whether you'll have the actual cash to service the debt. Here's the calculation:

$$\frac{\text{cash flow}}{\text{current portion, long-term debt}}$$

If your expected cash flow is $50,000, and the current portion of your long-term debt is $5,000, you'd have a 10:1 ratio. If other businesses in your industry have a 7:1 ratio, then you probably can safely take on more debt. In this case, the higher the ratio, the better, because the more cash inflow you have in relation to the payments you must make, the easier it will be to make those payments. Naturally, not all of your cash flow will be available to make the required debt payments.

It's also worthwhile to take a long-term look at the relationship between cash flow and the current portion of your long-term debt. Let's look at some of the figures from Quality Plumbing.

Figure 6–5 charts three lines. The flat line that's marked with small squares and runs across at 8.50 shows the industry average for cash flow compared with the current maturity of a business's long-term debt (that's what Phil's going to have to pay this year on his long-term debt). Phil also plotted his company's historical average. In this illustration, Quality Plumbing usually has a ratio slightly higher than the industry average, and it's marked on this picture as the line with small diamonds on it that runs across the graph at 9.10. What this means is that Phil's business usually generates cash flow about nine times higher than what his company will need to service this portion of its debt.

This graph makes it easy to see that when Phil's company made its major purchases and increased its long-term debt payment, the ratio between cash flow and the current portion of that debt dropped lower than it had ever been for the business and also fell below the industry average. Way back then, Phil should have done something to move this ratio at least above the 8.50 industry average. It also seems obvious that the purchases didn't bring in more cash, at least not initially. Phil should determine if there are problems with that new pumping machine and/or the radios that are preventing them from adding to the business's cash inflow. If Phil is confident that the purchases will bring in more money, then perhaps he can ignore

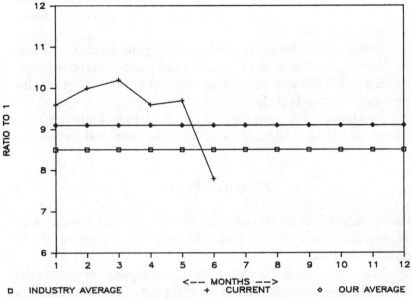

CASH FLOW / CURRENT MATURITY L.T.D.

□ INDUSTRY AVERAGE   + CURRENT   ◇ OUR AVERAGE

Figure 6–5 Line graph showing relationship between cash flow/current maturity and long-term debt.

this warning for a time. Otherwise, he should do something to improve his cash flow.

To summarize, you can avoid this kind of situation by taking certain steps. First, you track the information, so you know exactly where you stand in relation to your own historical trend as well as to that of others in your industry. Second, always do a profit analysis before you make any major purchase to make sure that whatever you buy will add to your company's profitability. After all, if something's not going to help your business make money, what's the point of buying it at all? Third, project your cash inflow, so you know in advance that you should be able to make any payments you take on.

Interest Payments

When Phil asked his banker to finance Quality Plumbing's truck purchases, the banker calculated a ratio that Phil wasn't even aware of. It's called the *times interest earned* figure and represents the amount of cash a company earns compared with the interest payments it must make.

This ratio gives your banker a feel for how capable you are of handling the interest costs you're now responsible for and also how much more debt you might be able to take on. It's a measure of how leveraged your business is.

To calculate the times interest earned figure, divide your earnings before interest and taxes by your total yearly interest expense. If you earn $20,000 and have interest costs of $1,000, your times interest earned ratio is 20:1.

Your banker will compare your ratio with that of others in your industry, including, if he has the available data, your local competitor.

Return on Equity

It's also useful to calculate your return on any investment you're planning to make to see if you'll make a profit or simply acquire something you'd like to have.

The top section of Figure 6–6 details a company's expected sales and return on investment figures for two years. The bottom section presents two different scenarios: one in which you make 25% of the total investment in the business and another in which you make only 15% of the investment into the company.

It's obvious that your return on investment will be greater the less cash you put into the business, but often how much difference it makes, on a percentage basis, isn't as evident. Your return will change as you use more borrowed funds, as there will be more interest expense involved, but you'll almost always be ahead if you can use more of other people's money in your company. In this illustration, a $10,000 loan made by others raises your company's first-year return by more than 50%, from 20% to 33%.

You might consider delaying payment to your suppliers, and running more of the "loans" you make through accounts payable, as there are no associated costs (like interest on borrowed funds). Often discounts are allowed when you send these suppliers a check, making this approach even more attractive.

The worksheet shown in Figure 6–6 is a very basic one you can use to determine your return on an investment. You want to include every source of leverage as you detail your figures. As always, there must be a happy medium between the amount of leverage you take on and what you're capable of handling. Your banker will consider

```
---------------------------------------------------------------
:                                                             :
:            Investment analysis worksheet                    :
:                                                             :
:    Projected sales:      1st year         2nd year          :
:                        ------------------------------       :
:                          200,000           225,000          :
:        less:                                                :
:        direct costs      140,000           160,000          :
:        overhead costs     55,000            55,000          :
:                        ------------------------------       :
:                                                             :
:        net profit                                           :
:        before taxes       5,000            10,000           :
:=============================================================:
:                                                             :
:    Our investment          $   25,000                       :
:    Investment from others  $   20,000                       :
:    Accounts payable        $   30,000                       :
:    Loans                   $   25,000                       :
:                               ----------                    :
:        total invested      $  100,000                       :
:                                                             :
:    return on our         1st year         2nd year          :
:    investment:             20%              40%             :
:-------------------------------------------------------------:
:                                                             :
:    Our investment          $   15,000                       :
:    Investment from others  $   20,000                       :
:    Accounts payable        $   35,000                       :
:    Loans                   $   30,000                       :
:                               ----------                    :
:        total invested      $  100,000                       :
:                                                             :
:    return on our         1st year         2nd year          :
:    investment:             33%              67%             :
---------------------------------------------------------------
```

Figure 6-6 Investment analysis worksheet.

how much you and how much outsiders have invested in your business.

Debt and Worth

The more leverage a company uses—the more debt it has in relation to what it's worth—the more vulnerable it is to changes in business conditions, especially those on the downside. One thing the business owner often forgets is that when he gets too leveraged, he might find himself in a position where he can't improve but can only get worse.

Here's an example: Let's say you start a business and it begins to grow rapidly. You expand mainly through the use of more supplier loans (accounts payable), some bank loans (that you're paying off by the month), and so on. After not too long a time, all of your working cash gets tied up in inventory, accounts receivable, and work in progress. You have to buy several trucks and more equipment to keep up with your expansion, so you have a number of monthly payments to make. Your cash flow is sufficient to handle your obligations, but it's starting to get stretched.

You're doing a terrific business, but all of a sudden you find that you're short of cash. So you start to borrow money for working capital, usually on a short-term basis (perhaps 90-day notes). You're able to pay off these loans as they come due. Then the opportunity comes along for you to buy a building at a good price. You do so, adding a lot to your long-term debt but not too much to your monthly costs. After several years in business, you have reached the limit of what you can do with your assets.

Based on your sales and the profit you've been recording (you've been putting a lot back into the business, of course), you're about as leveraged as your bank will allow.

But then let's say a new opportunity develops for your company; perhaps, if you're in one of the construction trades, a huge housing development opens right outside of town. Since you don't have the working capital to take on this additional volume of business, you look for a few outside investors. You have to offer them a pretty good return on their money to interest them, and a couple of them even insist on taking second mortgages on your building to hold as collateral for their loans to you.

So far, things look good; your business is in a situation that many others find themselves in. But where do you go from here? If business starts to stagnate just a little—if you don't get as much work from that new development as you expected, if more competition opens up, if interest rates rise a bit and construction drops off slightly—you're liable to find yourself in a very tight position from a cash standpoint. Your creditors—and these include the bank, your suppliers, and outside investors—don't care if things don't roll along as you thought they would. They're only interested in receiving the monthly payments you promised.

What's happened is that you've put your business into a position where it can't go anywhere but down. The upside potential is suddenly gone (unless something drastic happens, like one of your competitors closing his doors). While your company may continue to provide you with a decent living, it can't grow any further. You've overleveraged it.

The easiest way to avoid this situation is to constantly monitor the amount of debt your company has in relation to its value. Here's the formula:

$$\frac{\text{total liabilities}}{\text{tangible net worth}}$$

This ratio shows you the relationship between the capital you've contributed to your business and the amount of outside investment. The higher the figure, the more outside creditors have contributed to your company, and so the more highly leveraged the business is. The lower this ratio is, the more borrowing power you have; as this figure rises, the less likely it is that you'll get any loan you apply for.

This data is also listed in the *Annual Statement Studies*, which lets you compare your own situation with that of others in the same industry. As with cash flow compared with the current portion of your long-term debt, it's useful to chart this data over time. It'll give you a moving picture of your leverage condition.

Tips and Guidelines

Try to control the leverage your business uses by clearly marking leveraged items (both cash received and payments made) on your budget. Pay particular attention to the section of your balance sheet that details your long-term debt. Even though it shows what you're most interested in—the current portion due—you should be aware of the total debt you're responsible for.

Consider selling your accounts receivable. Sure, you'd have to offer these dollars at a discount, but they would give you immediate cash. Should you be carrying accounts receivable at all, letting your customers use leverage on you? Should there be a billing charge to help pay for the extra costs associated with carrying the accounts? More and more businesses add a service charge just to help pay for the extra paperwork it takes to handle accounts receivable, and customers don't seem to mind. Why not give it a try in your business?

Make a concerted effort to determine if you'd be better off with short-term rather than long-term leverage. You can usually come up with a more accurate forecast about what's going to happen over the next few months than you can over the next few years, and so you'll know better whether you'll have any problems in making the payments you take on.

You can also examine the ratio that compares your cash flow with the current portion of your long-term debt by adding any personal expenses to the cash flow part of the equation:

$$\frac{\text{net income + personal expenses + depreciation}}{\text{current portion of long-term debt}}$$

This adjustment almost always increases this ratio and gives a more accurate measurement of how cash flow can handle the current portion of a company's long-term debt. Personal expenses are discretionary, which means they're not vital to the profitable operation of the business, and a good portion of them can be eliminated. If times get hard, the cash that the business owner now spends on his personal things—a car is a good example—could be used for debt service.

Note that whichever way you calculate the cash flow/current portion of your long-term debt ratio, only a portion of what your business owes is included in the debt total. Another way to use this ratio is to include *all* debt that's due during the next year or operating cycle. This much harsher look at your financial picture will almost always lower the ratio.

Some analysts add in your lease payments to the current portion of your long-term debt to make the comparison even more accurate.

Another way to evaluate your times interest earned ratio is to add depreciation to the operating income part of the equation:

$$\frac{\text{operating income + depreciation}}{\text{interest expense}}$$

Since depreciation is a noncash expense, it lowers your cash condition. If your operating income really reflects the cash your business receives, which it must over a long period of time, then adding in depreciation will give you a more accurate picture of your cash flow. If you have a significant amount of depreciation during a period of time, changing the way this ratio is calculated can have a dramatic impact on the ending figure. Ask your banker which way the bank prefers to have this figure calculated.

7

Cash Grabbers: Inventory and Receivables

The biggest investment most business owners make is in their inventory. The second-largest place they invest their cash is in accounts receivable, those "loans" they make to some of their customers in an effort to make it easier for them to buy. What's funny about this—or maybe not so funny—is that when you started your business, you probably didn't intend to even have accounts receivable. But you often get forced into it because your competition allows its customers to charge at least part of their purchases, and for you to work in the same market, you have to provide the same service. Or perhaps it's traditional for the type of business you're in—people just expect it. Or, maybe you allow it because you discovered it creates more sales volume.

Whatever the reason, don't be surprised if you end up loaning part of your cash to those "good" customers. And realize that when some of them don't pay, it will play havoc with your cash inflow in exactly the same way as nonmoving inventory.

There's no question that the best policy is simply to insist that purchases be paid for when each job is completed, but in actual practice, it never quite works out this way. Some people will insist that you allow them to charge part of what they buy from you. Others will ask if 30 days is the the same as cash, and then not always pay in full when the 30 days have passed. Still other customers will tell your service people, "I always charge it," and put them in an awkward position. This is particularly a problem if you take over an existing business; it will already have some customers who charge what they buy, and they'll expect the same privilege from you. Others will want you to finance their purchases, and still others will tell you they'll write a check when the work is done, and then forget to send one or remit only a partial payment.

What can you do? After all, it's better to get something than nothing at all, and, in fact most of these people will pay—eventually. In many cases, you can charge interest on these pay-by-the-month accounts, which increases your profit and helps pay for the money you have to borrow to finance your accounts receivable. In effect, then, try to start with the best of intentions—ask everyone to pay cash for everything they buy—but then don't be surprised when that doesn't work 100% of the time.

The Complications of a Growing Business

When you first started in business, it was pretty easy to tell where your investment was. You could see it sitting on your shelves, knew to the penny how much you had spent for equipment and office supplies, and had a single-page list of customers who owed you money and how much they had charged. But as your company grew, so did your cash control problems. Your inventory ballooned, sometimes without enough thought given to what you were buying. Things hung around in your stock, getting more worn and less salable as each day went on.

All of a sudden you have work in progress, which gobbles up payroll dollars and adds to your accounts payable total *before* you can bill your customers. Many times you don't receive all the invoices for a particular job until that installation is long completed and billed, so you often don't know what kind of a gross profit you made on the work until way too late to do anything about it. Tickets for "extra" work aren't always billed on time, which creates customer complaints. You find each customer pays in a different manner when you allow them to charge their purchases—some when they receive the bill, others at the first of the month, and, sadly, some not at all. As a business expands, control of your inventory and accounts receivable becomes ever more important.

As you grow, it becomes more complicated to evaluate your data. Inventory is listed on your balance sheet at cost; the figures usually don't take into account what you lose from breakage or theft, the decreasing value of your inventory as styles change and some of your products become obsolete, or any markdowns of your product line as a result of changing competition. Accounts receivable are listed on that same balance sheet on a retail basis, but the numbers do include a deduction for anticipated bad debts. This percentage may or may not be accurate.

Demanding Down Payments

The whole idea when you work with accounts receivable and/or inventory is to move cash faster through both areas. It's surprising how a small change in the way you handle either part of your business can make a significant difference in your cash flow. For example, for years my company sold its furnaces and coolers to people without asking for a down payment; anyone could call up and order something and we'd do the work and then we would send a bill when we completed the job. As the end of each month approached, we hustled to get the bills in the mail before we ran out of cash.

I finally realized that people don't really expect to buy anything without putting some money down, and so I started to ask for a down payment that covered at least my material costs. That way, if the customer was slow to pay, my out-of-pocket expenses were taken care of. Asking for a down payment may seem like an obvious policy, but thousands of small companies let people charge their entire purchase and send out bills at the end of the month (instead of when the work is completed). A few slow-paying customers—and we all get them—start to really hurt. Several more of these folks who only promise to pay and a company can go down the drain even though it's doing a terrific sales volume.

As a rule, try to get as much cash in advance as possible. Insist on a down payment from every client, and include in each contract or estimate form whatever percentage of the total you'd like up front. Don't make exceptions. You'll be amazed at how the cash you collect in advance will improve your cash flow.

Aged Accounts Receivable

The quality of your accounts receivable is determined to at least some degree by their age. You're much more likely to collect an account that you just sent an invoice to than one that's 120 days old, and so the former is of better quality. Generally, if you have an inventory item in stock for longer than normal, it gets shopworn and is more difficult to sell for its full price. Normal conditions naturally decrease the value of your receivables and inventory, so the more current should make up the largest percentage and the oldest should be your smallest. Let's examine a typical small business and see where its dollars get stuck.

Roger, the owner of Nuts & Bolts Hardware, has 80% of his investment right on his shelves as inventory. He lets some customers charge what they buy, so most of what's left of his cash is out as accounts receivable. Just lately, though, things have taken a turn for the worse. Two major discount stores have recently opened, including one that specializes in small hardware. The other handles many of the same items that Roger does. Both stores, because they're connected to national chains, buy in volume, and thus sell for less. The only way Roger can compete with them is to offer better, personalized service and to allow all his customers to charge what they buy.

Since the larger stores carry a wider variety of stock, Roger decides he must expand his inventory. The increase cuts into the amount of cash he has available to support accounts receivable, though, so he finds himself in a quandary. The more he allows people to charge their purchases, the less money he has to add to his inventory. And if he spends what working capital he has to expand his inventory, he won't be able to allow charge accounts.

Like most businesses, Roger's company is becoming more complex as it grows. His larger inventory is more difficult to control; more acounts receivable mean that more people don't pay when they promise they will.

Figure 7–1 shows what might be the normal distribution for Nuts & Bolts Hardware's aged accounts receivables. This particular breakdown is done in more detail than usual (the standard breakdown is done at 30-day intervals); it breaks down the aging accounts into more categories and in 15-day increments. The greater detail often makes it easier to spot a deviation in the figures and shows you exactly where you stand. It also helps you understand and get a feel for the numbers and makes problem areas easy to spot. With just a few old receivables, it should be easy for you to pinpoint the exact accounts you need to contact. Finally, a graph like the one shown in Figure 7–1 is the beginning of a historical record for your business, the start of the database, so to speak, against which you'll

Age of accounts receivable

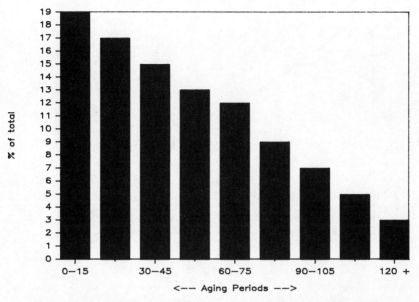

Figure 7–1 Column chart showing age of accounts receivable.

compare future information. As your records grow and get more involved, it's vital that you have some common ground on which to
make comparisons. As you continue to add information to your
records, the pictures you see will have more and more validity and
will make it easier to spot any deviation from the norm. For example,
the largest percentage of accounts should be those that are the most
current, followed by those that are 30–45 days old, and so on; the
oldest accounts should make up the lowest percentage of your total
accounts receivable.

A column chart gives you a good feel for the size of each of the
percentages. If Roger were to plot a line across the top of these figures,
its highest point should be the upper-left corner, and it should drop
steeply to the lower-right corner. This would make it easy to see if
any of the figures are higher or lower than what he would expect
them to be.

Figure 7–2 plots just the line for Roger's data, without the bars
underneath it. Now it's even easier to spot any deviation from the
falling line; as you can see from the slight blip in the line, the 60–75
day area is a bit higher than it was expected to be.

One way to begin following the age of your own accounts

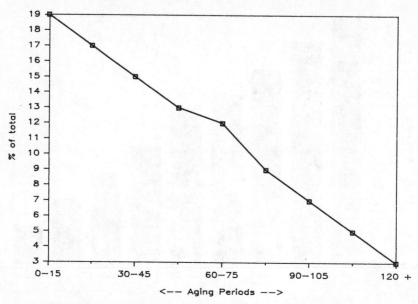

Figure 7-2   Line graph showing age of accounts payable.

receivable is to use the simple worksheet shown in Figure 7-3. It takes just a few minutes to fill in the blanks, but it will give you a good picture of the status and quality (or lack of quality) of your accounts and also indicate any deviations from your normal percentages.

The secret to any successful accounts receivable system is to collect an account just as it turns old—but before it starts growing

```
:---------------------------------------------------------------:
:                                                               :
:  Accounts receivable aging worksheet                          :
:                                                               :
:  Month:   August                                              :
:                                                               :
:                                                               :
:  Aging          % in this      % usually in     difference    :
:  Period         category        this category     + / -       :
:                                                               :
:  Ø - 15      [   12   ]      [   15   ]      [    3    ]    :
:  15 - 30     [   37   ]      [   32   ]      [    5    ]    :
:  30 - 45     [   30   ]      [   35   ]      [   -5    ]    :
:  45 - 60     [   10   ]      [    8   ]      [    2    ]    :
:  60 - 75     [    6   ]      [    6   ]      [_____]    :
:  75 - 90     [    2   ]      [    1   ]      [    1    ]    :
:  90 - 105    [    Ø   ]      [    Ø   ]      [_____]    :
:  105 - 120   [    3   ]      [    3   ]      [_____]    :
:                                                               :
:---------------------------------------------------------------:
```

Figure 7-3   Accounts receivable aging worksheet.

whiskers. The best advice on how to handle aging accounts is perhaps the oldest: Remember that the squeaking wheel gets greased. Have you ever fallen behind on payments, perhaps let a couple of your credit cards get a month or two late? That happens to everyone, and when it does, who do you pay first? The credit card company that writes you several notes or the one that has someone call up and ask you when you can send them a check?

Similarly, as a customer edges a bit past the payment terms you agreed to, you should call him and ask for a commitment on when payment will be made. There are all kinds of cute notes and reminder letters available, and sometimes they work, but it's always the company that has someone call that collects more of its accounts receivable.

Keep in mind that the phone call should be a polite reminder. You might even suggest that the business might be at fault and say something like, "Possibly you didn't get our statement." Sometimes a simple inquiry asking if the work you did was satisfactory will produce results. The customer *knows* what you're calling about, and nine times out of ten he'll mention the bill before you do and commit himself on when a check will be sent.

Speeding Up Your Collection Period

The cash you collect—and the dollars you don't—varies according to the length of your operating cycle, and many companies don't understand theirs. As you may recall from Chapter 2, your *operating cycle* is the time it takes your company to complete its average transaction: The time, for example, that elapses from the moment you make a sale, then order the equipment for the job and do the work, to the moment you collect from the customer. The standard rule of thumb is that an operating cycle is about a year, but as we saw in Chapter 2, for many companies, that's not true. Here's the formula:

$$\text{operating cycle} = \frac{\text{average collection period}}{+}$$
$$\text{inventory turnover rate}$$

Let's review how to use the operating cycle equation. The first part of the equation computes how long it takes you, on average, to collect for a sale once it's been recorded into your accounts receivable system. Go back through your records for whatever period you want to examine and average your month-end accounts receivable totals.

You also need to calculate your credit sales figure—how much you charged, during the period under study, through accounts receivable. Let's say you charged $144,000 and your average month-end accounts receivable totaled $12,000.

If you divide your total credit sales ($144,000) by your average accounts receivable total ($12,000), you get an answer of 12. This means that you generated and collected money through your receivable system 12 times during this year—an average of every 30.4 days.

As you track these figures in your own company, always keep in mind that if you can somehow speed up the movement of dollars through your inventory and/or your receivables, you'll be more profitable and improve your cash flow. Let's say, for instance, that you were able to reduce your average collection period by 20%; instead of taking (in this example) an average of 30 days to collect your cash, you take 24 days. You would have more money available sooner, which lets you do more business, which in turn creates more profit. You can plot your average collection period to get a better feeling for its movement over time.

Figure 7–4 plots Roger's old accounts receivable over the last nine months. It's easy to see that his accounts that are over 40 days old have been growing slightly and now come to a bit more than 12% of his total accounts receivable. His old receivables average is 9.3%, so Roger's suddenly taken a major move in the wrong direction. Whether this ratio is high or low depends, of course, on a particular business, as each company is different. The point here is that only by examining these old accounts can a business determine if more of its accounts are aging or if people are really paying on time.

What can you do about slow-paying customers? As mentioned earlier, the easiest thing is to simply get after the people whose accounts are aging *before* those amounts get too old. Set up a system that follows through immediately when someone gets a bit late on a payment. For example, if you allow charge accounts on a net-30 basis, send your nonpaying customers a reminder note immediately after the 30 days have passed. If 45 days go by, call and ask if there's a problem. Don't forget the grease-the-squeaking-wheel principle.

OLD ACCOUNTS, LATEST 9 MONTHS

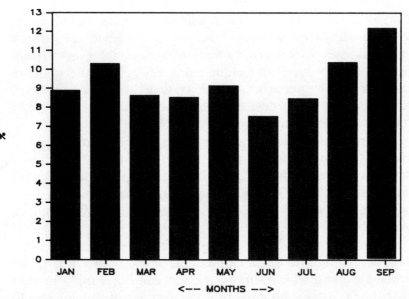

Figure 7–4 Column chart showing old accounts.

If your customers have learned from experience that your company will let its accounts slide a bit, you won't be first in line for payment when they get some cash in their hands.

You also need to screen credit applications as thoroughly as possible. For years my company did business as many smalltown firms do: We trusted everyone. These days that's simply impossible. Perhaps just asking for a credit reference or two, rather than demanding an entire formal credit application, is enough. In that case, make sure one of the credit references is the customer's bank, and call and talk to his or her banker. Ask the bank—and any other references—these questions:

> How long has Mr. So-and-so been your customer?
> How much credit does he have available?
> How does he normally pay?
> Does he discount your bills?
> How much does he owe you now?
> Has he ever missed a payment?
> Would you let him charge a purchase again?
> Any other comments about this customer?

The Cost of Customer Loans

You lose money on each invoice that doesn't get paid, and it's useful to fully understand how much sales volume it takes to just get back to a break-even point. In most situations, because things are so competitive, it's impossible to include a percentage in your markup to allow for those customers who won't pay, so when someone does stiff your company, where does the cash come from? Unfortunately, it comes right out of any net profit your business produces.

Here's an example. Not long ago, Nuts & Bolts Hardware picked up a big account—a new homebuilder who told Roger that his construction company would make all its hardware purchases at Roger's store. He knew Roger's prices were a bit higher than the chain stores but liked Roger's service and the convenience of charging all his purchases.

They had a good relationship for about a year, and then the homebuilder skipped town. He owed Roger $500 when he left, and Roger was just glad it wasn't more. How can Roger make up that loss? If he's working on a net profit percentage of 5%, Roger will have to record another $10,000 in sales to make up for the $500.

What is your actual accounts receivable total and how do you calculate it? Consider that it isn't the full amount; after all, you buy material and labor at wholesale and sell it at retail; the retail sum is what's charged through your accounts receivable system. For $1,000 worth of sales volume, your actual cost might be only $700 (that's assuming a 30% markup). But your cost really isn't just the $700; you still have to pay your overhead: utilities, phone, rent, and so on. If your direct cost percentage is 70% and your overhead is 25% of sales, 95% of every sales dollar you record is already spoken for and must be paid. You'll be left, if everything works as it should, with a net profit of 5%.

What this means is that for every $1 you let customers charge through your accounts receivable system, you've got to come up with 95¢ in cash to pay for both your direct costs and the overhead expenses associated with the sale.

Time also affects your actual costs. Let's say you do some work for a customer on Monday, and let her charge the total of $100. You won't have to pay for any labor involved in this sale until payday at the end of the week. If your labor costs total $30, your out-of-pocket expenses so far are $30.

Now, you've got a good relationship with your suppliers, so that you don't have to pay for the material you purchased for this job for another 30 days. Those costs—the rest of your direct costs—are $40. If the customer pays you before the 30 days are over, only the $30 for labor comes out of your working capital. If the customer hasn't paid you before your supplier's invoice comes due, the other $40 will have to come out of your working capital.

If you're short of cash, you might also miss a supplier discount because the customer didn't pay within the 30 days she promised she would. Furthermore, you must pay the overhead costs that are part of this job, almost always within thirty days. Perhaps during the first week, the phone bill came due, and a couple of weeks after the sale was made, the light bill had to be paid. That amounts to an additional $25 (25% of the $100 sale).

As you can see, if the customer doesn't pay within 30 days after the job is completed, you'll have to come up with 95% of the sale total to pay your bills. That's the amount you end up loaning the customer. Your profit, if any, arrives with her final payment.

Figure 7–5 is a grid that details how much money it takes to allow customers to charge their purchases through an accounts receivable system. It shows the cash required at varying profit levels to maintain different amounts of accounts receivable.

For example, if your company expects to allow $25,000 to be charged through its accounts receivable system, and the business works with an average net profit of 7%, it will need $23,250 in cash

```
              <-- Amount charged to accounts receivable -->

              $15,000    $20,000    $25,000    $30,000    $35,000
             -------------------------------------------------------
          1 : $14,850    $19,800    $24,750    $29,700    $34,650 :
          2 : $14,700    $19,600    $24,500    $29,400    $34,300 :
          3 : $14,550    $19,400    $24,250    $29,100    $33,950 :
          4 : $14,400    $19,200    $24,000    $28,800    $33,600 :
          5 : $14,250    $19,000    $23,750    $28,500    $33,250 :
Expected  6 : $14,100    $18,800    $23,500    $28,200    $32,900 :
net       7 : $13,950    $18,600    $23,250    $27,900    $32,550 :
profit    8 : $13,800    $18,400    $23,000    $27,600    $32,200 :
percentage 9 : $13,650   $18,200    $22,750    $27,300    $31,850 :
         10 : $13,500    $18,000    $22,500    $27,000    $31,500 :
         11 : $13,350    $17,800    $22,250    $26,700    $31,150 :
         12 : $13,200    $17,600    $22,000    $26,400    $30,800 :
         13 : $13,050    $17,400    $21,750    $26,100    $30,450 :
         14 : $12,900    $17,200    $21,500    $25,800    $30,100 :
         15 : $12,750    $17,000    $21,250    $25,500    $29,750 :
             -------------------------------------------------------
```

Figure 7–5 Worksheet showing amount charged to accounts receivable.

to pay its direct and overhead costs. This is the figure at the intersection of 7% on the left (profit) side of the grid and $25,000 on the top (sales) side of the illustration. If it expects to have $35,000 in sales and works on a profit of 4%, it will need $33,600 in cash to support these customer "loans." What's surprising are the large amounts required to let people charge their purchases through an accounts receivable system.

This particular illustration covers amounts from $15,000 to $35,000, in $5,000 increments, and uses net profit percentages from 1% to 15%. If you make such a grid for your own company, you would naturally want it to reflect the dollar and percentage amounts you expect to carry through your accounts receivable.

Can you afford any more accounts receivable? Some businesses do a terrific sales volume and get all their working cash bogged down in receivables; they get into trouble when some of their customers don't pay. Think carefully about how much cash you have available for customer loans, and be cautious about who you extend this credit to. How deeply would you look into their credit rating if you were going to write them a check for 95% of what they requested? Often, you don't think of credit sales as real dollars, but they are, and you're the one who has to come up with the cash.

Hidden Receivables

Many businesses don't realize how much cash they have tied up in what's called work in progress, or when they can expect to receive the money. For some companies, this cash doesn't amount to a whole lot, but for others, whose work takes a longer time, the amount is considerable.

Roger, for example, got into the habit of keeping a running ticket for his larger customers. He would just add each day's purchases to their sales slip and wouldn't calculate its total or send it out until the end of the month. The idea was to cut down on his paperwork, but he actually hurt his cash flow by delaying the time that great amounts of money were brought in. Whether or not you've been paid for work, you must pay your employees on time. And you often have to pay for the equipment and materials you've used on a job long before it's completed. Part of this problem can be eliminated by partially billing your clients as parts of a job get done. This is a common practice in the construction trade, in which companies also tend to request a down payment before starting the work.

Most customers will immediately pay a partial invoice, particularly if it details the costs of materials, labor, and so on. They've budgeted the money—most will already have it in the bank—for the work.

Do you have work in progress? Is payment sometimes held back because a part didn't arrive in time or was damaged when you received it? Do you have work in the mill that's partly done but has not been billed? If so, send out these billings right now.

Lowering Your Inventory Turnover Rate

As you may remember from Chapter 2, the second step in figuring your operating cycle is to calculate your inventory turnover rate, which tells you how fast your inventory, on average, is sold and taken out of your stock. You can do this for any period of time, but to keep it simple, let's work with yearly figures. Let's say that your cost of goods sold figure (from your projected year-end balance sheet) is $100,000. Let's also assume that you carry an average inventory of $25,000.

If you divide your cost of goods sold ($100,000) by your average inventory ($25,000), you get an answer of 4, meaning that you turned your inventory an average of 4 times during this year. By dividing the 365 days in a year by 4, you'll find that you moved your inventory an average of every 91 days.

If you carried an average inventory of $10,000 during this same period, you would divide the cost of goods sold ($100,000) by $10,000, which gives you an answer of 10. When this is divided into 365 days, it tells you that you moved your stock every 36.5 days. Naturally, the faster you can move products through your inventory and collect for them, the more profit you will make, as you're turning your money more and more.

When you combine your turnover rate with your average collection period, it tells you that your business had an average operating cycle of about 121 days (91 days to move the stock off your shelves plus 30 days to collect for it once it's sold).

There are a number of ways to examine the turnover rate of what you sell, but the place to start is with a basic list:

Item	Average turn rate	Turn last 60 days	Turn last 6 months	Turn last year
Screen door #1	42	45	47	47
Screen door #2	42	51	50	51
Screen door #3	42	40	41	42

This chart tells you that screen doors turn, or sell, an average of every 42 days. The one that stands out here, of course, is door number 2, as it was selling slower than normal last year, produced the worst sales during the past six months, and has been selling at an even slower rate during the last 60 days. As always when analyzing information, watch for any variances from the norm; in this case, pay attention to what's starting to sell slower than it has historically. That way you can often spot things that are going out of style, that you may have priced too high, that the competition is marketing more aggressively, and so on.

Figure 7–6 is an inventory turnover worksheet you can use to compare what you expected to happen in your inventory with your actual figures. To help you get a feel for what items are selling, the worksheet is broken down by departments.

```
              Inventory turnover worksheet
 ---------------------------------------------------------
 :                                                         :
 :                                                         :
 :                      Expected      Actual     Variance  :
 :   Department         turnover      turnover   + / -     :
 :                                                         :
 :                                                         :
 :  [ Retail    ]      [ 40 ]        [ 43 ]      [ 3 ]     :
 :  [ Plumbing  ]      [ 40 ]        [ 46 ]      [ 6 ]     :
 :  [ Wholesale ]      [ 50 ]        [ 55 ]      [ 5 ]     :
 :  [ Metalwork ]      [ 38 ]        [ 44 ]      [ 6 ]     :
 :  [ Contracts ]      [ 40 ]        [ 43 ]      [ 3 ]     :
 :  [_____]       [    ]        [____]      [___]     :
 :  [_____]       [    ]        [____]      [___]     :
 :  [_____]       [    ]        [____]      [___]     :
 :  [_____]       [    ]        [____]      [___]     :
 :  [_____]       [    ]        [____]      [___]     :
 : ------------------------------------------------------- :
```

Figure 7–6 Inventory turnover worksheet.

The most significant figure you get from this worksheet is the variance amount: how much more or less rapidly your inventory moves through your company than you had anticipated. This gives you valid information on the quantity and timing of your orders.

It's also a good idea to examine product groups in this same way. You might discover, for example, that your screen door section is selling at a much slower pace than the rest of your hardware items. You would want to find out why—have you selected a poor product? Is it priced too highly? Should you have a sale to clear out the section?

The best thing about lowering your inventory turnover rate is that it frees cash for other purposes—such as creating more business.

How to Picture Your Turnover Rate

It's always a good idea to look at your turnover rate over a long period of time to try to get a feel for where it's been and where it's heading. While it's usually impractical to create a chart for every individual item, it's worthwhile to examine your turnover rate for the business as a whole. For example, if you find your inventory turnover rate is growing, that means the number of days you have things on hand is stretching out, which will in the end lower sales and slow down cash—and thus will decrease your working capital. It's like aging your accounts receivable: If it's taking you longer to collect for your work, you have less cash to do business with.

Figure 7–7 shows how often, in days, Nuts & Bolts Hardware turned its inventory over a 48-month period. To create a graph like this, calculate your inventory turnover rate every month and mark it on the chart. A line graph gives you a good feeling for the movement of the data.

Let's take a look at the data in Figure 7–7. At the start of the period, Roger took about 34 days to turn his average inventory item. By the end, though, he was taking more than 40 days to do the same thing. Naturally, some items will sell much faster than others, and some won't be sold at all.

The chart will help you determine how much you should have in stock given your sales volume. In most companies, where inventory items make up the largest part of the sales total (there may be some labor or other things that add to total sales volume), there's a direct relationship between the number of goods on hand and the sales that are made: the more inventory, the more sales. For many companies, however, it gets to be something of a chicken-or-egg situa-

AVERAGE DAYS TO MOVE THE INVENTORY

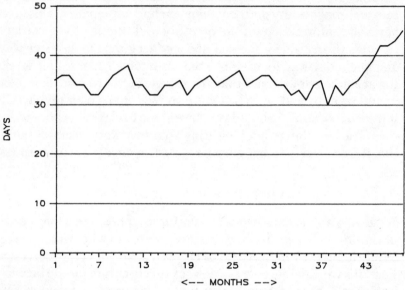

Figure 7–7   Line graph showing average days to move the inventory.

Turnover rate by department

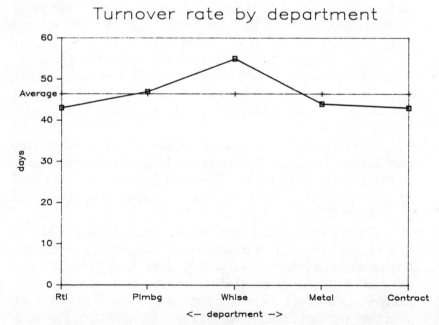

Figure 7–8   Line graph showing turnover rate by department.

tion: Does more inventory create more sales, or do more sales enable the business to put more in stock simply because there's more cash to support inventory purchases? The bottom line, of course, is that if you don't have it in stock, you're not going to sell it.

An effective way to get a line on how much you should have in inventory is to examine your sales records and chart the data over time. You'll discover that the degree that inventory influences sales varies according to the type of business you are in and within companies in a given industry.

Usually, the general rule—the more inventory, the more sales—holds. If not, the selection of things you had for sale and their prices were not right.

Figure 7–8 is a line chart that details the inventory turnover for the different departments of Nuts & Bolts Hardware. It's an easy graph to put together, as all you need to calculate are the turnover rates for each section of your company. As you can see from the chart, for some reason things aren't moving through the wholesale end of Nuts & Bolts as fast as they are through the rest of the company. Why not? Does that department handle products that always move slowly? Is its product selection getting less effective? Is its pricing structure out of line with the competition?

Once you find a variation in one section of your company, you've got to determine why the department or division is operating differently from the others. There may be a good reason for any change you discover, but you should be aware of it.

Another good idea is to check each department or division's inventory sales on a square-foot basis. You might learn that while one part of your company carries a huge inventory, the sales it makes on a square-foot basis are right in line with those recorded by the rest of the business. You might also discover a particular department or area that seems to have weak sales volume but really doesn't once it's examined on a square-foot basis. Or you might find that one department is selling much better than the others and increase your investment in inventory for that area to see if a rise will cause a corresponding jump in sales.

The Importance of Monitoring Inventory

After Roger successfully handled the loss of a major customer, he found the situation in his city changing. A big plant outside of town closed, eliminating about 5% of the community's jobs, and the area's other major employer won a union contract calling for severe wage decreases. To make things worse, another hardware store opened, threatening Roger's little business with a smaller slice of a shrinking pie.

Seeing the handwriting on the wall, Roger does his best to cut back. He lays off some part-time help and puts in more hours himself but keeps three employees. He grudgingly scales down his newspaper and radio advertising budget, knowing it will hurt in the future but he must consider his present needs. He watches every penny the business spends for utilities, phone calls, and repairs, taking a lot of time going over his check register to track each of his expenses.

But at the same time, he's locked into a lease he can't break, an advertising contract with the Yellow Pages that calls for a specific monthly amount, and enough fixed costs that he can see he's got major problems. He gets a bit behind on his payroll taxes (had to use the money to make payroll) and finally digs into his personal savings when the IRS insists on payment.

What do you think happens to the company's inventory through all of this? It almost always starts to drop, not just as a percentage of total sales, but as a raw-dollar figure. When the electric utility sends a shut-off notice, the business owner must use whatever cash is available to keep the lights on rather than to replenish inventory.

In cases like this, inventory, which doesn't call and ask for a check, gets something of a short shrift and starts to drop, which hurts sales even more, which in turn causes inventory to drop further until it's too late. The lesson for every business is that it must monitor its stock on hand, both in dollars and as a percentage of sales, to really know what's happening to the company.

Tips and Guidelines

Where else might cash jam up in your business? Do you order a lot of special items for your customers and often have to pay for them long before you collect? Do some people order things and never pick them up, much less pay for them? Do you do a lot of work on spec, meaning you may or may not get paid in full? How might you change these practices to make sure you get at least your cost for the work you do or the parts you order? All it takes is a company policy that insists on payment in advance for any special-order item. Bigger companies do this (Sears is a good example), and it makes sense for smaller businesses to follow their lead.

In addition to examining each individual aging step, it's also worthwhile to look at your accounts receivable information in terms of its *average* age. How old is the average account you carry? Is your average getting older, or is it improving? You would naturally want to see a decline in the average age of the accounts you have: If it starts to increase, it's cause for concern.

Since the older accounts are the main ones you have to worry about, it's useful to track what percentage of your total accounts receivable is old. *Old* in the context here is anything older than your normal collection period. In other words, if you ask for full payment within 30 days, you should expect that most of your customers will send a check within that time.

Why not sit down and track a dollar as it moves through your company? Where does it really move, and where does it sit? How long does it get stuck here or there? Once you learn where your cash sits, you can devise ways of moving it along.

How do your merchandise displays affect your sales? Do you find that advertising increases sales of an item and also raises sales in other areas? Would it make sense to advertise whole sections of merchandise, rather than just one item from each area? Create a link between your advertising dollars and your sales total, and constantly compare the two. Try different time frames for this; you might find that the advertising you do today won't have an effect on sales for one month or six weeks or two months or more.

Put a specific credit-reporting procedure into place, and call people when they're even a bit late at paying you.

Can you help your cash flow and collection period by financing everything you sell instead of carrying your own paper? Do you have access to enough cash to set up your own finance company and buy the accounts receivable from your business? If you do this, your company will get its cash (discounted slightly, of course) and your finance company can collect interest on what is owed.

Can you get whatever you sell on a floor-plan or consignment basis? This would cut down your inventory investment and give you more cash to do other things.

Create a standard inventory rotation/pricedown procedure, so that when something's been in your stock for a specific period of time, it's automatically reduced in price. This helps keep your cash flowing.

Track down what's happened to your working capital since you started your company. It should total your original investment plus any retained earnings your company has earned, less any dividends or other special bonuses it has paid. How much is now invested in inventory? Accounts receivable? Fixed assets? How much is in the form of cash?

If your business is growing, the year-end inventory total on your balance sheet may give you a false reading of your inventory turnover rate; it might be lower than what you really have been experiencing. You'll usually have a higher inventory at the end of the period than you did at the beginning, simply because your sales will be higher than they were at the start. Rather than using your ending inventory figure to divide into your cost of goods sold amount (to calculate your inventory turnover rate), first calculate your *average* inventory for the period, then divide it into your cost of goods sold total.

You can do this one of two ways. You can add your beginning inventory total to your ending inventory figure and divide by two. Or you can add up your month-end inventory totals, if they're available, and divide by 12 (months).

Some analysts suggest that you divide your average inventory into your sales figure instead of into your cost of goods sold total. However, since you carry inventory on your balance sheet at cost, keeping everything on a cost basis gives you a more accurate reading of your turnover rate. (Since your inventory is at cost, it should be divided into another cost figure, in this case, your cost of goods sold.)

Calculate your *days inventory ratio* by dividing your ending inventory figure by your average daily cost of goods sold (you calculate your daily cost of goods sold by dividing your total cost of goods sold figure by 365). This figure represents the number of days you can go without replenishing your inventory and also tells you the average time period that your dollars are invested in inventory.

Here's an example. Let's say you have a year-end inventory total of $25,000 and your cost of goods total for the year was $250,000. If you divide $250,000 by 365 (days), you end up with 685. When your inventory is divided by 685, you get 36; that's how many days it usually takes you to completely run out of inventory if you don't replenish it. It also means that your capital is stuck in inventory, on average, for 36 days.

8

A Look at Your Future: Break-Even Analysis

Tracy's Boutique is a small dress shop. Tracy has only two employees, so she doesn't have a large payroll, and almost all of her assets are tied up in her inventory. She rents the building she works out of and has been in business for three years. During that time, her company's shown a paper profit, but Tracy's had a hard time figuring out where her profit is. She's taken enough out of the business to live on, but it's still a struggle to make ends meet. Her business is all-cash, so her main concern is determining how much sales volume she must do to at least break even.

There's an old story in business that if you break even, you'll never go broke, and it's true: You don't have to make money to stay in business, you just can't lose money. Many companies get into trouble because they're unable to determine their break-even point, so they don't know how to price things, what sales to realistically expect, and so on.

If you're just starting in business, you have nothing more than an educated guess as to what your sales will be next month, much less next year. It's equally hard to determine costs in advance. There always seems to be something—often many things—that messes up your best projections.

Every business is different when it comes to its costs, expenses, and sales, yet most methods that help a company determine its break-even point are tailored to manufacturing enterprises. These methods call for adding your total costs and dividing them by the number of units you expect to manufacture or sell; the result is the price you must put on each unit to break even. Anything over and above the break-even point creates a profit. Most small businesses are retail or a combination of retail/service enterprises, and the technique they use to determine their break-even point is slightly different.

Your break-even level is related to three things: your sales volume, fixed expenses, and variable costs. Variable costs, also called direct costs, vary directly with your sales volume. If sales increase, direct costs rise along with it and vice versa.

While sales are reasonably easy to estimate, the other two items in your calculations aren't always as clear. It's necessary to understand what a fixed cost is and what a variable cost is and apply the definitions to your own company. There's not much help here from outside sources, either, as your break-even point is so individual that it applies only to your own business.

Types of Costs

A *fixed cost* is something you have to pay whether or not you sell anything; rent and utility expenses are examples. A *variable expense* is one that varies by the sales you make. For example, what Tracy's Boutique pays for merchandise is a direct variable cost because it will vary according to the company's sales. The more dresses it sells, the higher sales will be and the higher variable costs for that merchandise will be.

Generally, the more you sell, the more material you'll purchase. Even this gets confusing at times, though, as things don't always vary at the same rate. For example, your sales may increase 5%, but the direct labor needed to support those sales might go up only 4%, or the material used for the items sold might jump only 2%. Part of this is because you record sales at their retail price and labor and materials at what they cost you, but it's also because nothing changes at the same rate as sales, which are always handled on a retail basis.

Calculating Your Break-Even Point

Why use a chart to determine your break-even point? The best reason is that a graph makes the figures easy to see and understand, especially when you compare a number of possible scenarios. You might want to experiment with various markup levels and/or fixed cost totals. A picture of each of the different approaches will make understandable images out of any number of worksheets filled with data.

The normal break-even graph plots at least three lines—one for costs, one for sales, and one for profits—and many add another line to represent fixed expenses. Unfortunately, all these lines make the whole process seem more confusing than it really is.

Also, when you create your break-even chart, the scales won't be what you normally see on a graph. Usually, business graphs plot information as time-series data. The period of time the graph covers is normally shown on the horizontal scale, with months (or quarters, or years, or whatever) running left to right ← → across the bottom of the picture. The vertical (up and down) scale usually represents size or value; the higher a line or bar is on the vertical scale, the larger the number it's intended to represent.

A break-even graph, however, charts the same scale on both axes. Since a break-even chart is designed to show where costs exactly equal sales, both scales must increment equally: Sales and costs must go up or down at constant rates of change.

Break-even graphs are not designed to display past data. They are used for one specific purpose: to give a business a visual image of exactly the point at which it will break even under a particular set of circumstances. To do a break-even analysis of her company, Tracy starts with the following assumptions:

> Her monthly sales range starts at $5,000 and increases to $15,000 in $1,000 increments.
> Her fixed costs are $3,000 per month.
> Her variable costs amount to 70% of total sales. For each $1 in sales she records, the cost of her inventory will use 70 cents.

Tracy's total costs, then, will be her $3,000 monthly overhead amount plus 70% of her sales volume. Here's a list of the information:

Sales	Fixed costs	Variable costs	Total costs	Profit
5,000	3,000	3,500	6,500	− 1,500
6,000	3,000	4,200	7,200	− 1,200
7,000	3,000	4,900	7,900	− 900
~	~	~	~	~
13,000	3,000	9,100	12,100	900
14,000	3,000	9,800	12,800	1,200
15,000	3,000	10,500	13,500	1,500

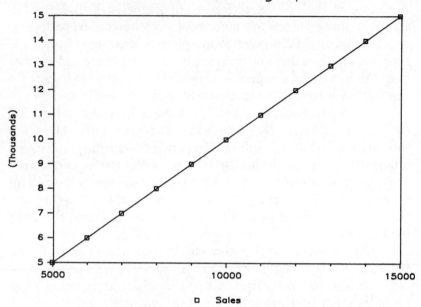

Figure 8–1 Break-even graph, showing sales line.

Within this range of data will be the break-even point for Tracy's Boutique. This is the kind of list you probably made before you started your company to get an idea of your own break-even point. You might have used several variable direct cost levels—71%, 72%, and so on—to determine what markup to adopt.

This information is usually more useful when you plot it. Tracy starts her graph with just one line, for sales. (When you do break-even charts for your own business, draw one line at a time. If you keep things simple, your pictures will be easier to understand.) Figure 8–1 plots Tracy's sales data, starting with her lowest assumed sales figure, $5,000 (in the lower-left-hand corner), and running to her highest amount, $15,000 (in the upper-right-hand corner). Next, Tracy adds her total cost line. The point at which it intersects with her sales line will mark her break-even point.

Figure 8–2 plots both the sales line (marked with boxes) and the total cost line (marked with plus signs) for Tracy's Boutique. Tracy's break-even point, at the cost levels specified ($3,000 in fixed monthly costs and a 70% variable cost), is $10,000 in sales volume.

Note that the scales for both axes are the same: They start at

Break—even graph

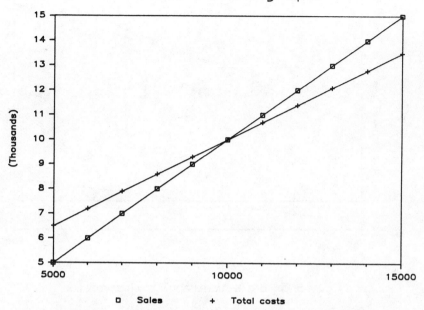

Figure 8-2 Break-even graph, showing added cost line.

$5,000 and go to $15,000. The difference between the two lines represents Tracy's profit or loss. Before the two lines met, she recorded a loss. Once they crossed each other, she made a profit.

Figure 8–3 adds the profit line (which is negative for a time) to the sales and total cost lines. The profit line, marked with small diamonds, crosses the zero line at exactly the same place the sales and total cost lines intersect. These three plots tell Tracy that her business will lose about $2,000 (the first profit plot) if it records sales of $5,000 and will make nearly $2,000 if it records sales of $15,000. The profit line will show as a negative until the business reaches its break-even point.

What if Tracy's variable cost rate rises from 70% to 75%? What if she cannot increase her selling prices while her direct costs jump to 75 cents of every sales dollar?

Figure 8–4 shows the graph Tracy's Boutique will create if its variable costs increase to 75% of its sales. This picture tells Tracy that an increase of 5% in costs causes a 20% increase in her break-even point—which is now around $12,000.

Break—even graph

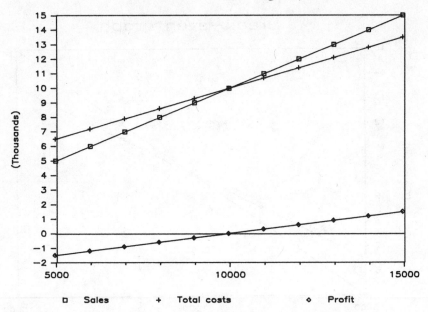

Figure 8-3   Break-even graph, showing profit line.

Break—even graph

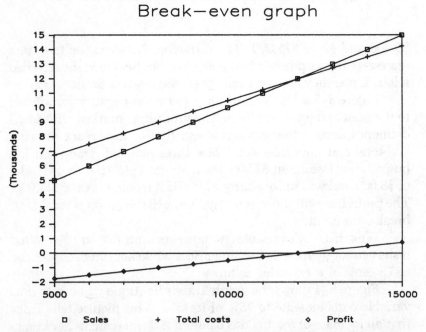

Figure 8-4   Break-even graph, showing profit line at different sales and cost levels.

Your Anticipated and Real Break-Even Point

One of the best things about break-even analysis is that you can use the information it produces to compare what actually happened with what you expected to take place. Tracy predicted that her break-even point was about $10,000 per month in sales volume, assuming monthly fixed expenses of $3,000 and a variable cost rate of 70%. But once she's been in business for a time, she'll have a more accurate idea of the sales her business must record.

Figure 8–5 plots the $10,000 break-even line straight across the chart at the $10,000 mark, as well as the actual sales and profit figures for Tracy's Boutique. This picture makes it easy to see when the business made a profit and when it did not. Tracy's estimates of her fixed cost and variable cost percentage were on target; when sales dipped below the $10,000 figure, the company lost money, and vice versa.

Although sales fluctuated wildly, ranging between $9,000 and $14,000, profits didn't move anywhere near as much. The reason, of course, is that profits are only a small percentage of sales (in this example they averaged slightly less than 4% of sales). You wouldn't

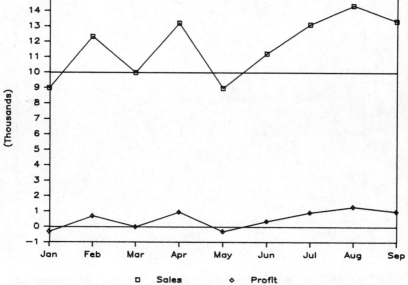

Figure 8–5　Actual vs. break-even line graph, showing dollar differences.

	Sales	Fixed costs	Variable costs	Total costs	Profit	Sales % change	Profit % change
Jan	8988	3000	6292	9292	-304	-23.32%	-158.80%
Feb	12332	3000	8632	11632	700	5.21%	35.49%
Mar	9983	3000	6988	9988	-5	-14.83%	-100.99%
Apr	13211	3000	9248	12248	963	12.71%	86.57%
May	8989	3000	6292	9292	-303	-23.31%	-158.74%
Jun	11212	3000	7848	10848	364	-4.34%	-29.58%
Jul	13122	3000	9185	12185	937	11.95%	81.39%
Aug	14332	3000	10032	13032	1300	22.28%	151.70%
Sep	13321	3000	9325	12325	996	13.65%	92.96%
Oct	[_____]	[_____]	[_____]	[_____]	[_____]	[_____]	[_____]
Nov	[_____]	[_____]	[_____]	[_____]	[_____]	[_____]	[_____]
Dec	[_____]	[_____]	[_____]	[_____]	[_____]	[_____]	[_____]
Average	11721				Average 516	Average .00%	Average .00%

Figure 8-6 Worksheet listing sales and expense details.

expect them to produce the same wild swings that sales do, and in dollar terms they cannot. Doesn't that mean, though, that even a minor change in sales can create a major change in profits? Let's look at the *percentage* changes in the data, rather than the raw figures themselves.

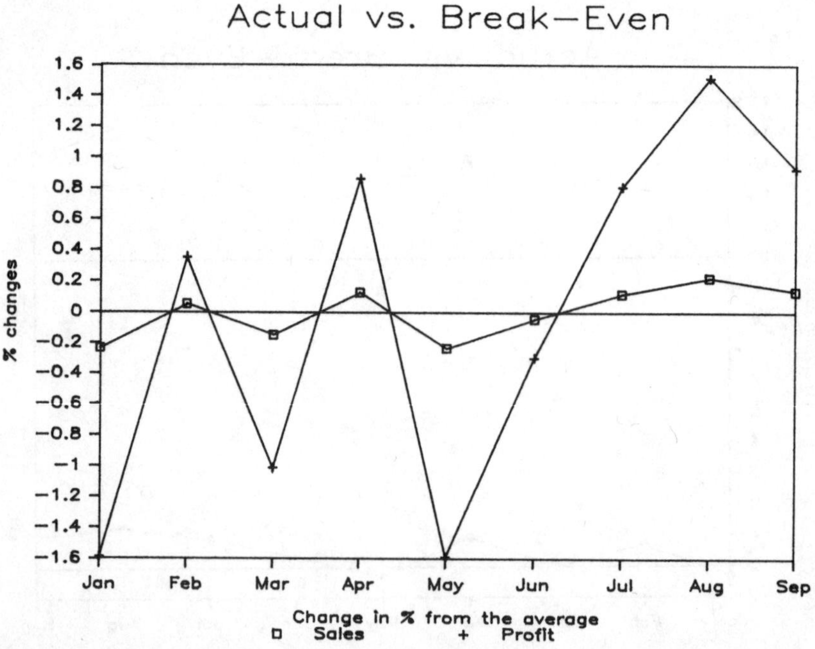

Figure 8-7 Actual vs. break-even line graph, showing percentage differences.

Figure 8–6 lists all of Tracy's data on her sales and expense items. The graph shown in Figure 8–5 plotted these sales and costs, along with her projected $10,000 break-even point. The two right-hand columns of Figure 8–6 show how, on a percentage basis, both sales and profits differed from the average. When you examine the percentage changes, you'll see that profits swing much more wildly than sales. Note, however, that they both have the same overall rate from a percentage standpoint.

In May, for instance, sales for Tracy's Boutique were $8,989, 23.31% lower than Tracy's average sales. Profits for that month, though, were –$303, or some 158.74% less than Tracy expected. At the same time, when sales and profits increased, from a percentage standpoint, profits always moved at a sharper rate. For example, August sales were up some 22.28%, while profits were 151.70% above average.

Figure 8–7 plots the percentage changes from the last two columns of Figure 8–6, and it's easy to see the wider swing in the profit end of things. The sales line is relatively calm. This tells Tracy that even a minor change in sales can cause a major change in profits from a percentage standpoint.

How Floor Space Changes Your Break-Even Point

Once Tracy knows her break-even point, she can relate it to other parts of her business. The downtown store she works out of has 2,000 square feet of display area. As far as her break-even level is concerned, each square foot of sales area must produce $5 in sales (Tracy's $10,000 break-even amount divided by 2,000 square feet). The figures she actually recorded, in Figure 8–6, show that her average is slightly higher. For the nine months listed, her average monthly sales were $11,721. So her present location is actually generating average sales of $5.86 per square foot.

How will these figures help Tracy if she decides to expand? Let's say she finds a location in the local shopping mall with exactly the same monthly fixed costs—$3,000. Her variable costs have remained pretty constant at that 70% rate, so it would appear that she would need the same sales volume—$10,000—to break even at the new location. But Tracy needs to consider one other thing. The store location in the mall has only 1,500 square feet of display area. When Tracy divides her break-even point by the number of available square feet, she finds that if she's to break even at the new location, she'll have to somehow raise her sales per square foot to $6.67, or about $1 a square foot more than she's currently recording. Can she do so?

She probably won't know for sure without trying, but in the meantime she can find out from other merchants in the mall, especially other clothing stores, their sales per square foot. Tracy might not get correct figures from some of her competitors, but she'll get an overall view that will help her decide whether to open the new store. Also, since many lease contracts at shopping malls require the tenant to pay a percentage of the company's sales to the owners of the mall, Tracy can probably get some sales-per-square-foot averages from the owners.

The Break-Even Point for a Service Business

Let's shift our focus from a purely retail store to a service business: Welding & Steel Inc. Walt, the company's owner, sells a few parts and some angle iron, but the bulk of his work is providing labor to weld things together, both at his shop and at the customer's place of business. He usually employs three people.

Walt calculated that his company needs $13,000 in monthly sales to break even. He charges $25 per hour for each of his three welders, bringing in daily sales of $600. That comes to $3,000 in sales per week, $13,000 per month, and $156,000 per year. Since these amounts are awfully close to the borderline of profit and loss, Walt figures that he'll do as much welding himself as he can, and that's where the company's profit will come from.

Walt wanted to impress upon each employee that he must bring in a certain amount each month for the company to break even. This is a difficult task, especially since, like most business owners, Walt doesn't want his employees to know exact profit and loss numbers, because they sometimes assume that the owner is getting rich off their labor and won't believe otherwise.

Walt broke down his break-even data into its simplest form to get the point across to his employees. He told them that for Welding & Steel Inc. to break even, each employee has to bring in sales of $25 during every hour worked. Walt decided to communicate this information, on a monthly basis, with a line graph illustrating the data. This way he can update the chart at the end of every month, and the welders will constantly know how they're performing. Shar-

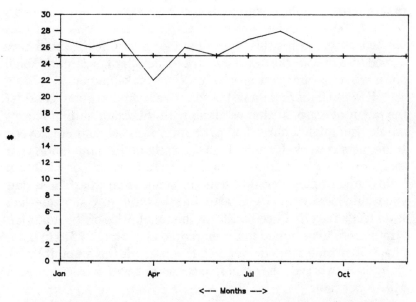

Figure 8-8 Line graph showing break-even point in dollars-per-hour.

ing this type of information also helps to maintain a good working environment; after all, everyone wants to know what's happening.

Figure 8–8 details Welding & Steel's sales over the first nine months of the year. The break-even point, $25 per hour, is also plotted as a straight line across the graph. Obviously, when the plot falls below that line, the business is losing money and vice versa.

One advantage of this approach is that actual sales and cost data are not released to the employees. It's also in a form that's easy to understand.

During the first three months, Walt's employees produced sales above the calculated break-even point, but in April, the sales per hour figure took a real plunge. As soon as Walt noticed the drop, he talked to his employees about it. Since they too can see the decline in the graph, they were interested in finding out why it occurred. Perhaps some jobs went sour, possibly poor scheduling resulted in a lot of wasted time, or an employee was paired with someone he couldn't work with effectively. Maybe there was a problem in the billing end of the business, and some jobs weren't properly charged out.

To use this chart for your own business, divide your total monthly sales by the number of hours your employees worked during that month. For example, if your sales were $50,000 and your employees put in 1,000 hours, they produced $50 in sales for every hour they worked. By gathering this type of data for several years, you'll have a good idea of your business's average dollars-per-hour figure. You'll learn what amount you need in order to make money.

If you sell more than just labor, it's also important to consider the factor of seasonal change along with this examination. For example, you might charge $30 per hour for one of your employees. If that person works for eight hours and sells nothing but labor, your total gross for this employee would be 8 hours × $30, or $240. But if this same employee installs something major on a particular day, you would have to add its value to the sales total. In Walt's case, let's say a truck rack had been built, so the retail price of the materials ($150) needs to be added to the employee's sales total: $240 in labor plus $150 in materials equals $390. If you divide this amount by the eight hours worked, the employee comes out with a sales figure of $48.75 per hour.

This tells you two things. First, you really can't study this data over a short period (a day or even a week), as the fluctuations will be too great. Even on a monthly basis, you'll show a lot of ups and downs. You need to compare the same periods for two consecutive years to get a valid picture.

Tips and Guidelines

If you have a specific production capacity (in total sales or number of units you can sell), compare it with your calculated break-even level. You might find that your employees can produce only a certain amount of business under even the best of conditions, and it may be under your break-even point. You might have to take on another line of whatever you sell.

Make break-even worksheets and/or graphs for the various divisions or sections of your company. Perhaps you'll discover that to make a profit you must sell much more of something than you realized, or you may learn about a product area that produces a better markup, which means you can sell less of it and still come out in the black (and naturally, you'd want to find some way to sell more of the product).

If your business is profitable at a certain sales level, you should determine how much sales can drop and still leave you at a break-even point. The difference is your *safety margin.*

Do a break-even analysis by product line, type of customer, or sales territory.

If you have a microcomputer, use a spreadsheet program to create worksheets that detail your break-even point down to the exact dollar for any number of different scenarios. The computer makes doing what-if analysis all that much easier.

Before you expand into a new area, or buy another company, plug your projected data into a break-even worksheet and graph. Act like you're just starting (which you really are with the new venture), and explore various percentage markup and sales levels.

If you have a good break-even condition (i.e., your business is operating at a higher level of sales than you need) include a break-even chart along with your financial statement when you ask for a loan. A chart that shows a wide safety margin will help you make your case with your banker.

Try applying break-even techniques to your larger jobs. For construction firms in particular, it's useful to look at all the costs associated with each project the company bids on to determine its break-even point.

9

How Fixed Assets Can Save—or Waste— Your Dollars

Superior Heating & Cooling is a retail sales and service business that concentrates on the installation of indoor comfort systems. Henry, Superior's owner, has one person in the office to do the books and answer the phone (he does the estimating himself), three sheet metal workers, and four service technicians.

Superior Heating & Cooling has six trucks, some machines to do its sheet metal work, and some smaller tools. The business just landed a contract to install the heating and air-conditioning systems in a number of homes to be built over the next few months. That put Henry in the market for a new slitter, which he feels will make cutting sheet metal faster and more efficient. Or will it? The slitter is what's called *fixed asset*—something a business purchases that has a specific, or fixed, cost. *Fixed* assets can be either productive assets (like a new piece of machinery) or nonproductive ones (a new picture for your office wall). You need things like desks and chairs, but they don't always make you more efficient. Perhaps you need trucks, machinery, and other equipment, and their condition and how well they suit your needs determine if they will make money for your company.

There are a lot of questions a business owner can ask about the fixed assets the company buys and has available to use but perhaps only one answer: If it doesn't make your employees more productive or increase sales in some way, don't buy it. But how can you determine that one purchase will be more productive than another?

Predicting Productivity or an Increase in Sales

Instead of just asking the company's banker for a loan to buy the slitter, Henry put down some figures on paper to help him decide whether to go ahead with the purchase.

Figure 9–1 is the worksheet that Henry used to calculate the company's current sheet metal cutout costs and to estimate costs with the new slitter.

Right now, Superior Heating & Cooling has a roller and a brake. If it buys the new slitter, it will have to make a new monthly payment of $800, but its maintenance costs should decrease, because the other, older machines will be used less. Current maintenance costs are $600 a month, and Henry estimates that they will drop to $400. Utility costs will increase $100 a month, as the new slitter will use more electricity. What was taking 600 labor hours per month will now take 500, so labor costs will drop from $8,910 to $7,425 (Henry's labor costs are about $14.85 per hour).

One thing Henry didn't take into account is that if he's right about his labor estimate, the business will have an extra 100 hours, about two and a half weeks of someone's time, to put to other use each month, which should increase its sales. Henry also must consider if the company can in fact increase sales or whether the purchase of the new slitter will mean that an employee will *lose* that 100 hours every month.

With its current method of cutting sheet metal, Henry's business wastes about 3% of its total material costs. For the upcoming work, that would come to some $900. With the new slitter, the waste will be only about 2%, or $600.

The worksheet shows that if the business buys the new slitter, its total costs will decrease some $1,085, or about 9%. Thus the slitter purchase makes sense.

This worksheet won't fit your business exactly, of course, but you can adapt it. Before you decide to buy an asset, sit down and do the same thing that Henry did: List all the costs and benefits of the new purchase, and calculate the bottom line. This will give you some numbers that either support the decision to buy or indicate

```
:---------------------------------------:
:                                       :
: Productivity Measurement Worksheet    :
:-------------------------------------- :
:             (Current)                 :
:-------------------------------------- :
: Monthly costs:                        :
:                                       :
: Equipment:                            :
:            Roller           $500      :
:            Brake            $200      :
:            Maintenance      $600      :
:            Utility costs    $750      :
: Labor:                                :
:      600 Labor hours        $8,910    :
:                                       :
: Material waste:                       :
:    3.00% of total           $900      :
:                          ----------   :
: Total cost                  $11,860   :
:                                       :
:=======================================:
:                                       :
:             (Estimated)               :
:-------------------------------------- :
: Monthly costs:                        :
:                                       :
: Equipment:                            :
:            Roller           $500      :
:            Brake            $200      :
:   (New)    Slitter          $800      :
:            Maintenance      $400      :
:            Utility costs    $850      :
:            Other          [_____]    :
: Labor:                                :
:      500 Labor hours        $7,425    :
:                                       :
: Material waste:                       :
:    2.00% of total           $600      :
:                          ----------   :
: Total cost                  $10,775   :
:                                       :
:=======================================:
:                                       :
: Total current:              $11,860   :
: Total estimated:            $10,775   :
:                                       :
: Dollar difference:          ($1,085)  :
: Percentage difference:      -9.15%    :
:                                       :
:---------------------------------------:
```

Figure 9-1   Productivity measurement worksheet.

it's not the right thing to do. It forces you to quantify things that you might otherwise not examine closely.

It's often hard to quantify some costs. Henry, for example, had to guess the number of labor hours the work would take with the new slitter, but he made an *educated* guess. Likewise, he knew his past maintenance costs for his old machinery but had to estimate them for the new slitter. You too will have to make educated guesses for things you can't quantify. What's important is to get all the figures down on paper.

You can also adjust the numbers to give you different results based on your estimates. For example, if Superior's labor cost dropped from 600 to 550 hours (instead of the 500 Henry estimated), total costs would decrease only $343, or slightly less than 3%. The new slitter might still make sense (after all, the savings will still be about $4,000 a year), but Henry should look a little harder at the data. If his estimates of cost savings in other areas (maintenance and waste) are incorrect, then the slitter purchase may be a bad buy.

Keep in mind that for some purchases, you'll have to factor in increased insurance or storage costs. Or perhaps labor hours will be spent getting the machinery installed and on line. All these things will help you decide whether sales will actually increase or productivity will really improve.

The Effect of a New Asset on Sales

As already discussed, the idea behind buying most assets is to increase either productivity (and thus lower costs) or sales. Henry's slitter wouldn't do a thing for sales, but it would help cut costs. Other machinery might increase sales, but it usually takes some time before the impact of the new sales starts to be felt. Henry's got the chance to purchase a computerized ductwork machine to speed up the production of sheet metal ducts. It will cost about $10,000 a year; the monthly payments are $800.

Figure 9–2 outlines Superior's current sales and cost figures and its estimated figures with the new machinery in place. The sales column reveals that Henry's business is busiest during the summer months, with July and August recording the largest sales volume.

Henry figured his current costs at 74% of sales. If the company buys the new machinery, the monthly payment of $800 will increase costs to about 75% of sales. Overhead, in both instances, is calculated at $15,000 per month. The second column on each side of the worksheet adds the overhead and the direct costs.

The last column on each side of the worksheet lists net profit before taxes, and it's obvious that high sales during the summer months provide much of the profit for Superior Heating & Cooling.

```
!---------------------------------------------------------------!
!  (Current)                          (Estimated)               !
!  Overhead = $15,000 / month         Overhead = $15,000 / month!
!  Gross costs are 74% of sales       Gross costs are 74% of sales!
!                                     plus $800 per month for    !
!                                     the new payment            !
!                                                                !
!---------------------------------------------------------------!
```

	Sales	Direct Costs Plus Overhead	Net Profit Before Taxes	Sales	Direct Costs Plus Overhead	Net Profit Before Taxes
Jan	70,000	66,800	3,200	70,000	67,600	2,400
Feb	70,000	66,800	3,200	70,000	67,600	2,400
Mar	70,000	66,800	3,200	70,000	67,600	2,400
Apr	70,000	66,800	3,200	70,000	67,600	2,400
May	80,000	74,200	5,800	85,000	78,700	6,300
Jun	90,000	81,600	8,400	95,000	86,100	8,900
Jul	100,000	89,000	11,000	110,000	97,200	12,800
Aug	110,000	96,400	13,600	120,000	104,600	15,400
Sep	90,000	81,600	8,400	100,000	89,800	10,200
Oct	80,000	74,200	5,800	85,000	78,700	6,300
Nov	70,000	66,800	3,200	75,000	71,300	3,700
Dec	70,000	66,800	3,200	75,000	71,300	3,700
Jan	70,000	66,800	3,200	75,000	71,300	3,700
Feb	70,000	66,800	3,200	75,000	71,300	3,700
Mar	70,000	66,800	3,200	75,000	71,300	3,700
Apr	70,000	66,800	3,200	75,000	71,300	3,700
May	80,000	74,200	5,800	85,000	78,700	6,300
Jun	90,000	81,600	8,400	95,000	86,100	8,900
Jul	[_____]	[_____]	[_____]	[_____]	[_____]	[_____]
Aug	[_____]	[_____]	[_____]	[_____]	[_____]	[_____]
Sep	[_____]	[_____]	[_____]	[_____]	[_____]	[_____]
Oct	[_____]	[_____]	[_____]	[_____]	[_____]	[_____]
Nov	[_____]	[_____]	[_____]	[_____]	[_____]	[_____]
Dec	[_____]	[_____]	[_____]	[_____]	[_____]	[_____]
	$1,420,000	$1,320,800	$99,200	$1,505,000	$1,398,100	$106,900

	Dollars	Percentage
Increase in sales:	$85,000	5.99%
Increase in costs:	$77,300	5.85%
Increase in profit:	$7,700	7.76%

Figure 9–2   Current vs. estimated overhead worksheet.

The new purchase—if Henry's estimates of sales are correct—will add $7,700 to Superior's business over the next 18 months, or 7.76% more in profit before taxes. Like the slitter, this purchase makes good business sense. But if Henry's sales estimates are not on target, the business may have a problem.

Henry can also use this worksheet to do some what-if calculations. He can enter different sales levels until he determines his breakeven point for this purchase. Once he knows it, he can judge whether sales will increase enough to justify the purchase.

Henry probably can get some information about how sales might increase from other businesses that own a computerized ductmaking machine. Trade industry magazines might also provide insight on how well the equipment works and whether the sales increase Henry has projected is valid.

Henry calculated that it would take four months for the new machinery to increase sales. For the first third of the year after the business bought the new equipment, he assumed that sales would remain the same. Henry made his estimate by figuring out when the profit with the new machinery would equal the profit without it. He did that by creating a graph.

Figure 9–3 plots Superior's cumulative profit before taxes using both the current and estimated data. The current condition (without the new purchase) is shown as a solid line; the estimate is represented by a line marked with small plus signs. The graph makes it easy to see that until about July, Henry's business would have recorded a larger profit without the new machine than with it. Later, the two lines start to separate; the profit level, with the new machine, intersects the original line at the end of July and passes it. From that point on, the business will make more profit with the new machine than it would have without it.

This data tells Henry that if his estimated costs and sales projections are correct, the business will have a lag of about seven months

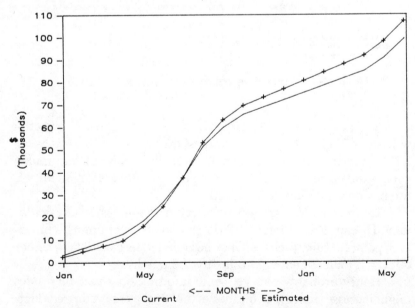

Figure 9-3   Cumulative profit before taxes line graph.

before profits will be equal. During this time the company will have to get by with less cash, as it will produce smaller profits. But once this period is over, the new machinery will raise profits.

Nonproductive Assets

Every company has some nonproductive assets, such as desks, chairs, and an office area. In most cases, you can figure that anything that makes your company more appealing to potential customers is a worthwhile asset; anything that doesn't help sales or reduce costs is not.

Some things, like microcomputers, are hard to quantify. If you've owned a PC for a time, you know that it probably didn't eliminate anyone from your office staff and thus didn't save you any money in that respect. It does, however, provide more information much faster and in more understandable ways (graphs are a good example), keep track of your data more accurately, let you do more, and so on. You're more effective as a business owner because of your computer, and this saves money, but it's often hard to measure the impact that such machinery and equipment have on your bottom line.

Using Assets Effectively

In a very real sense, how effectively you use your available assets determines your total sales, your ability to make a profit, your cash flow, and so on.

The danger with fixed assets is that it's easy to put too many dollars into their purchase (or lease payments). This inhibits doing business because it removes working cash from the total dollars your company has to do business with and can become a continuing problem: You still have to send in a payment every month for that machine you bought that didn't make your company more productive.

Chapter 4 examines and discusses two asset management ratios that focus on sales produced by assets. You can also get a good feel for how well you're using your assets by comparing their value with your profit.

Figure 9–4 lists four quarters' worth of information for Superior Heating & Cooling. During the first two quarters, the business had

```
!-----------------------------------------------------------------!
:                                                                 :
:                  Profit before taxes / total assets            :
:                                                                 :
:                  Profit              Total                      :
:                  Before taxes        Assets    Percentage       :
:                                                                 :
: First quarter        12,000          100,000       12.00%       :
: Second quarter       12,000          100,000       12.00%       :
: Third Quarter        12,000          110,000       10.91%       :
: Fourth quarter       16,000          110,000       14.55%       :
:                                                                 :
!-----------------------------------------------------------------!
```

Figure 9-4   Profit before taxes/total assets worksheet.

$100,000 in total assets; during the third quarter, it somehow raised its asset base to $110,000. Since these figures represent total assets, without regard to any liabilities the company has, the increase could have come from several sources: a cash loan or investment into the business, an increase in inventory, the purchase of a piece of machinery. In any event, the business was producing a $12,000 profit, or about a 12% return on its total asset base, during the first half of the year.

Although the business had more assets to work with during the third quarter, it produced the same profit it did during the first two quarters. That means that the new assets, whatever they are, are not working for the business or at least not yet.

The company's profits jumped during the last quarter of the year, although it didn't increase its assets during that period. The increase in assets that occurred in the third quarter apparently began to yield profit for the business during the last quarter. If Henry had increased the company's inventory, it's now selling and creating cash. If the increase in assets came from a new piece of machinery, it must now be on line and cutting costs or making Henry's employees more productive.

Track this same information for your own company over time. Compare it with your own average and that of the industry you're in; you can look up this ratio (percent profit before taxes/total assets) in the *Annual Statement Studies.*

Your Percentage of Fixed Assets

In addition to knowing how well your assets are performing, it's useful to keep tabs on the percentage of your assets that are fixed assets.

```
:---------------------------------------------------------------------:
:                     Percentage of total assets                      :
:                                                                     :
:                                                                     :
:            Cash & cash          Accounts   Fixed            Total   :
:            equivalents  Inventory Receivable  Assets  Other  Assets :
:(last year)                                                          :
:1st qtr       17.00%      33.00%    32.00%    17.00%  1.00%  100.00% :
:2nd qtr       18.00%      34.00%    30.00%    16.00%  2.00%  100.00% :
:3rd qtr       17.00%      35.00%    29.00%    19.00%  0.00%  100.00% :
:4th qtr       18.00%      33.00%    30.00%    19.00%  0.00%  100.00% :
:                                                                     :
:(this year)                                                          :
:1st qtr       17.00%      32.00%    28.00%    22.00%  1.00%  100.00% :
:2nd qtr       16.00%      33.00%    26.00%    25.00%  0.00%  100.00% :
:3rd qtr       15.00%      34.00%    25.00%    26.00%  0.00%  100.00% :
:4th qtr    [_____]   [_____]   [_____] [_____] [_____][_____] :
:                                                                     :
:---------------------------------------------------------------------:
```

Figure 9-5   Percentage of total assets worksheet.

Fixed assets are made up of dollars that are invested in machinery or land or equipment or vehicles—things with a specific, fixed cost. Obviously, dollars invested in fixed assets are no longer available to help support your inventory, accounts receivable, or overhead; the cash is *fixed* in place, so to speak. It's also helpful to compare your current position with your past one and with that of similar companies in your field.

Figure 9-5 lists some calculated percentages for Superior Heating & Cooling. All the figures shown, as indicated, are divided by total assets to show as a percentage of that total. It's necessary to work with your figures on a percentage basis so that you can see any changes in where your asset dollars are being spent.

Since the data is in percentages, it's easy to think of it in relation to $100. At the end of the first quarter of last year, Henry's business had $17 in cash, $33 in inventory, $32 in accounts receivable, and so on.

Since all the columns add up to 100%, when one figure changes, so must another. In other words, when you add to your inventory (on this percentage basis), another asset as a percentage of the total must decrease. And likewise, if your accounts receivable decrease as a percentage of your total assets, then one or more other asset account must increase.

Henry graphs his asset information to obtain a useful moving picture of his business over the last four quarters.

Figure 9-6 plots all four data sets for the seven quarters of information listed in Figure 9-5. While a line graph with this many lines isn't easy to interpret, Henry can tell several things about his

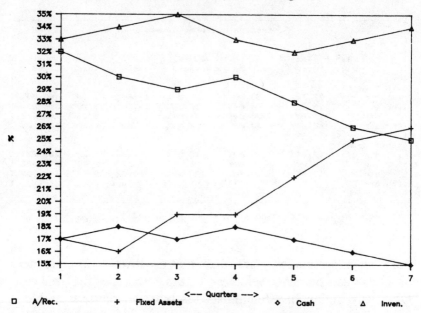

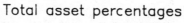

Figure 9-6 Total asset percentages line graph.

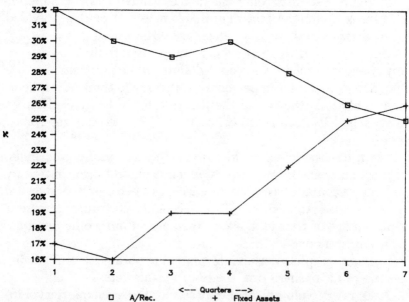

Figure 9-7 Total asset percentages line graph, showing only receivables and fixed assets.

operation during this period. He can tell, for example, that his inventory as a percentage of total assets has remained pretty stable. The highest line on the chart, it's been averaging about a third of his total assets. It's marked on the graph as a line with small triangles.

The second highest line on the chart, marked with small boxes, represents Henry's investment in accounts receivable as a percentage of his total assets. For some reason this line has been falling, especially since the start of the current year.

The line marked with plus signs represents Henry's investment in fixed assets. It's something of a mirror image of his accounts receivable percentage, as it's been rising for the past year. Over the last quarter, this line crossed the accounts receivable line and now shows that Henry has more of his total assets invested, on a percentage basis, in his fixed assets than he does in accounts receivable.

The lowest line on this graph, marked with diamonds, represents the percentage of total cash assets. This line has remained reasonably stable, although it's been falling slightly for three quarters of the current year.

Because it has so many data lines, this graph isn't especially easy to read or understand. However, it tells Henry where he might take a closer look. Since it seems to establish a relationship between the percentage of investments in accounts receivable and in fixed assets, let's examine these areas and eliminate the inventory and cash lines from the picture.

Figure 9–7 plots the accounts receivable and fixed asset percentages for the seven quarters shown. The dollars a business has in its receivables will eventually return to it as cash. Fixed assets, on the other hand, don't come back as cash unless they increase productivity. Even then, it usually takes much longer for fixed assets to return cash to the company, just because of the nature of the asset. A return of cash is certainly what Henry intends here, but should he rob money from accounts receivable to try to achieve that result?

For the first year, fixed assets as a percentage of total assets rose slightly, from about 17% to 19%. At the same time, the amount spent on accounts receivable dropped about 2%. Henry's investment in fixed assets rose from the first quarter of this year and now the business has more invested in fixed assets than it does in accounts receivable. That's where the two lines cross.

In effect, Henry's business, especially for the first three quarters of this year, has taken money from its accounts receivable and put it into fixed assets on a percentage basis in relation to total assets.

Perhaps there's a good reason that this happened. Possibly Henry decided that the business was having problems with its receivables and wanted to lower them. Perhaps the company let fewer of its customers charge than it has in the past. But if that were the case, then Henry's cash account would increase as accounts receivable fell (the business would have collected for more of its sales).

The danger here, if it continues, is that when Henry's business must add to its inventory, raise cash to fund a big job, or do business with customers who won't buy unless they can charge their purchases, it will find that it has so much tied up in fixed assets that it can't handle the change in its business pattern. As any area, as a percentage of total assets, starts to rise, another asset will start to fall. Where can Henry's company rob the cash from? If it wants to maintain its inventory level, and can't or doesn't want to sell off some of its fixed or other assets, the extra dollars needed to fund the increase in receivables will have to come from the cash reserve.

This image is not disturbing if the business's total assets, as a dollar figure, are growing rapidly. If this is the case, each section of the company has more dollars available for use, even though its percentage investment may change. As always, it's important to compare your current investment in fixed assets with your own past and with that of other businesses in your field.

Employees as Assets

What's your most important asset? Your employees—the person who answers your telephone, your best salesperson, your top installation crew. Business owners often don't consider people to be an asset and so don't think about how they might use them more effectively. But given that your employees are the ones who use your fixed assets, their quality is directly related to how well those assets perform.

In Superior Heating & Cooling's service department, the technicians use trucks, some expensive testing equipment, a welding set, a small crane, and other fixed assets. One thing that Henry does to get a line on how well his employees are performing is to track the callback rate of his service technicians and to consider it part of their labor cost. He charges the callback time to the technician who was originally on the job, no matter who goes back to fix it correctly. (A callback is when a service technician has to return to a job because whatever he repaired isn't working properly.) Some service technicians have a very low callback rate; others, for one reason or another, seem to generate customer callbacks.

By keeping track of callback rates, Henry can deduct a total cost for every employee and measure how well each is performing. Henry calculates the callback amount by taking the total monthly callback cost charged against each technician's jobs and dividing it by the number of working hours in the month.

Here's an example. In four weeks, there are 20 working days, or 160 working hours. During this month, Ed, one of Henry's service technicians, did calls that required five hours of callback time. Henry pays each service employee $14 per hour; by the time all the fringe benefits and tax costs are added in, each technician costs the company $19.50 an hour. Ed's total callback cost, for this month, is five hours at $19.50 per hour, or $97.50. When this is divided by the number of working hours this month (160), Ed's net callback cost per hour comes to 61 cents. Thus Ed, during the month under study, actually cost the company $20.11 per hour.

Figure out your exact costs over a year for each employee in your service department. Then total the sales you expect that employee to produce, and compare your employees on a gross profit basis. More often than not, the people receiving the highest salaries are the most productive. You might also learn that the employee in your service department with the lowest hourly wage rate actually has the highest rate after bottom-line costs have been figured. After you add in the callback rate, nonproductive time, and perhaps some training expense, low-paid people often cost a business the most.

Also consider how much you charge for retail labor and compare it with your profit. Add in your overhead costs and make a range of possible answers.

Figure 9–8 is a worksheet that Henry created to help his business understand the relationship between labor cost, number of service calls, and profit before taxes. Listed across the top of the worksheet are various retail labor rates. While Henry charges $31.50 per hour for his technicians, this worksheet is constructed to show him a range of figures.

Up and down the left side of the grid are various labor costs. These are the total of basic hourly rates plus fringe benefits and a range of callback rates and include Henry's 23% overhead figure.

The numbers inside the grid reflect Superior Heating & Cooling's anticipated gross profit for each hourly service call made by a service technician. By multiplying the number of hours each month

		<-- Retail labor rates -->					
		30.00	30.50	31.00	31.50	32.00	32.50
	25.32	4.68	5.18	5.68	6.18	6.68	7.18
	25.48	4.52	5.02	5.52	6.02	6.52	7.02
	25.64	4.36	4.86	5.36	5.86	6.36	6.86
	25.79	4.21	4.71	5.21	5.71	6.21	6.71
	25.95	4.05	4.55	5.05	5.55	6.05	6.55
Labor	26.10	3.90	4.40	4.90	5.40	5.90	6.40
cost	26.26	3.74	4.24	4.74	5.24	5.74	6.24
per	26.42	3.58	4.08	4.58	5.08	5.58	6.08
hour	26.57	3.43	3.93	4.43	4.93	5.43	5.93
	26.73	3.27	3.77	4.27	4.77	5.27	5.77
	26.88	3.12	3.62	4.12	4.62	5.12	5.62
	27.04	2.96	3.46	3.96	4.46	4.96	5.46
	27.19	2.81	3.31	3.81	4.31	4.81	5.31
	27.35	2.65	3.15	3.65	4.15	4.65	5.15
	27.51	2.49	2.99	3.49	3.99	4.49	4.99
	27.66	2.34	2.84	3.34	3.84	4.34	4.84
	27.82	2.18	2.68	3.18	3.68	4.18	4.68
	27.97	2.03	2.53	3.03	3.53	4.03	4.53
	28.13	1.87	2.37	2.87	3.37	3.87	4.37
	28.29	1.71	2.21	2.71	3.21	3.71	4.21
	28.44	1.56	2.06	2.56	3.06	3.56	4.06

Jan hours worked:	160	x gross of $		5.40	=	863.38
Feb hours worked:	168	x gross of $		5.55	=	932.40
Mar hours worked:	192	x gross of $		5.71	=	1096.32
Apr hours worked:	168	x gross of $		5.40	=	907.20
May hours worked:	168	x gross of $		5.71	=	959.28
Jun hours worked:	176	x gross of $		5.24	=	922.24
Jul hours worked:	160	x gross of $		5.55	=	888.00
Aug hours worked:	184	x gross of $		5.71	=	1050.64
Sep hours worked:	168	x gross of $	[_____]		=	[_____]
Oct hours worked:	168	x gross of $	[_____]		=	[_____]
Nov hours worked:	160	x gross of $	[_____]		=	[_____]
Dec hours worked:	168	x gross of $	[_____]		=	[_____]
		Average:		5.53		952.43
		Total gross:				7,619.46

Figure 9–8   Retail labor rate worksheet.

by the service technician's gross profit, Henry can determine how much he should make from each employee.

The worksheet in Figure 9–8 also lets Henry see some what-if figures: how much more (or less) gross profit would be produced at different hourly labor rates and/or different hourly costs. Henry can use this data to motivate his service technicians to cut their callback (and thus total) costs. It also gives Henry an idea of what would happen to his gross profits if he raised or lowered the service rates.

Figure 9–9 plots the average gross profit per hour for each of Henry's four service technicians. By tracking the data on a monthly basis, Henry creates a picture of how well his employees are performing. This example instantly shows that on average Ed makes the most for the business, while Joe has the worst average gross profit.

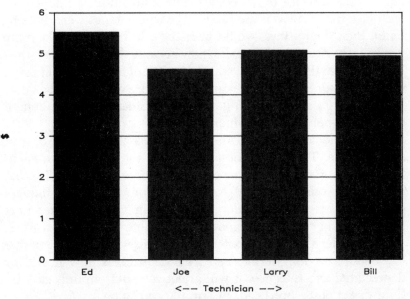

Figure 9-9   Column chart showing average gross per hour.

Tips and Guidelines

If your company uses a lot of expensive machinery, do a cost/profit breakdown for each piece of equipment. Figure out how much it's used per day, and try to work out a productivity rating for it. Add in its insurance and operating and maintenance costs, so you know exactly what it costs your business to have and use the equipment. Calculate your operational cost per hour.

Are there ways you could use your machinery more during every workday? Would that increase your profits?

Once you know exactly what each piece of equipment, machinery, or specific production technique costs your business, you can decide whether it makes more sense to continue doing jobs in house or to contract the work to another firm. Sending the work out would free some major dollars for your business, because you would no longer have to pay for some of your fixed assets.

Watch especially for labor-saving tools that don't end up helping your business. For example, my business owns a tool that makes cutting sheet metal much faster than doing it by hand. But who benefits from the use of this equipment? If my business charged the customer the same as it used to charge when things were done by hand, then the business would be helped, as it would make more profit. If the business charges less now because there's less labor time involved, then the customer gains the benefit of the equipment. Sure, my sales volume might increase because more work could be done, but the more important thing is for the business to get the benefit of its equipment and machinery.

Take a look at the fixed assets you have as a percentage of your sales volume. This calculation is listed in the *Annual Statement Studies*, which means you can compare your own results with that of others in your industry. By comparing your profit with those of companies listed in the *Studies*, you'll get an idea if it makes more or less sense for your own business to invest more or less in fixed assets.

Consider the type of potential fixed asset purchase: whether it's a short- or long-term asset. This determines how it will be depreciated and thus how it will affect your bottom line, cash inflow, direct costs, overhead, net profit, and so on.

Keep in mind that some of your fixed assets might be hidden assets. *Hidden assets* have been depreciated for some time and show a much lower book value than their real value. A building you bought some years ago is a good example of a hidden asset. It might be almost completely depreciated and have a very low book value but have increased dramatically in price. Hidden assets change your debt/worth ratio, as they can be added back to owner's equity:

$$\frac{\text{total liabilities}}{\text{owner's equity} + \text{hidden assets}}$$

The additional asset value makes the ratio drop. If you can add in the values of hidden assets, your business will look better in your banker's eye. It will appear to be a safer candidate for a loan, as it has more assets than shown on its normal balance sheet.

10

How Your Product Mix Determines Your Success

Central Construction Services (CCS) is a small business that gets its sales from four main places:

1. Wholesale, where the business records lumber sales, general hardware sales, and so on to building contractors;
2. Retail, where it sells construction products like paneling, two-by-fours, plumbing supplies, and so on to the general public;
3. New construction, where the company builds new homes for individual customers;
4. Old construction, where the business remodels older homes.

It might seem that each area of CCS mingles with all the others, and it does. But Kohl, the company's owner, designed a simple way to departmentalize its sales and costs.

First, each division of the company has its own set of books. Overhead is assigned on an individual basis to each section of the business. Rent for the retail store, which also services contractors, is broken down on a square-foot basis. Utilities are handled the same way. Management and other employee time is charged as it's spent; detailed time records are kept. Even Kohl keeps a detailed hourly time card, believing that employees who keep a time sheet become better at controlling their own time.

Second, each section of the company has its own particular color for its sales orders; that way, nothing gets confused. Employees are able to switch back and forth on the jobs they do and still keep track of where they spend their time. Costs are easy to monitor, too, with different sales orders for each department.

Third, costs are tightly controlled. Each invoice is immediately posted as it's received; when CCS employees purchase something from another business in town, they bring the invoice back to the office so it can be charged to the right department and sales order right then. Labor costs are posted to work in progress on a daily basis. Because cost records are always up-to-date, each department manager knows where things stand all the time. This is especially important for those in the construction business, who need to know, every day, how the estimated costs for each job in progress compare with actual costs. If 50% of the estimate has already been used, the work better be half completed. If it's not, there might be a chance to do something about it before it becomes a major problem.

Fourth, each department has its own office area, with rent, phone, lights, and so on charged to it. The office areas of the new construction and old construction parts of the company are the entire operation, since all these sections need is a small place to work on blueprints, estimates, and so on. The retail part of the business naturally has a higher overhead in terms of rent and utilities. The wholesale part of Central Construction Services, which has only two salespeople and one office employee and low warehousing costs, has the lowest overhead.

Allocating Your Costs

If you split your own company's work into logical divisions, you can also split the records you track. For example, if you have a retail-only store, you might want to distribute what you sell into sections. Overhead can be charged on a square-foot basis (e.g., if one part of the company's stock takes 40% of its showroom space and 40% of the office staff's time is spent on it, it should be charged 40% of the overhead). Also determine where you and employees spend your time, then charge it accordingly.

If you have a service department, keep its records, costs, and sales volume separate from those of all other parts of your business.

If you deal in any resale items (products that you sell to other people, who in turn sell them to someone else), keep separate track of their sales and costs. Every company has sections that can be departmentalized.

Analyzing Your Sales

CCS's involvement in a range of different areas gives it some protection from the business cycle. If times are good, more new homes will be built, so the new construction and wholesale end of the company should do well. By selling to other building contractors on a wholesale basis, the business can maintain its total sales volume even if its new construction section doesn't sell its share of new homes, because other contractors will, which helps CCS's volume.

When times get a little tough and new home construction drops off, people tend to remodel and fix up their homes rather than build new ones. The company can then concentrate on increasing sales in its retail and old construction departments.

Figure 10–1 is a detailed worksheet that Kohl uses every month and quarter to see where Central Construction Service's sales come from. In this example, sales for the first quarter total $240,000. Each section of the business is listed, including two areas—resale and service labor—that don't contribute a great deal. The worksheet also lists the average for each department of the company, along with any variance in the data. Knowing where your sales come from is the first step to increasing them.

About a quarter of Kohl's sales during this period came from the company's wholesale division. Retail sales accounted for slightly more than 20% of total sales, and new construction provided the highest percentage—some 27.08%.

```
:------------------------------------------------------------------:
: Sales breakdown. 1st quarter    Total sales:   240.000           :
:                                                                  :
:                          Amount   Percentage   Normal   Variance :
:                                                                  :
: Wholesale                57.000     23.75%      25.00%   -1.25%   :
: Retail                   50.000     20.83%      23.00%   -2.17%   :
: Construction (new)       65.000     27.08%      23.00%    4.08%   :
: Construction (old bldgs.) 45.000    18.75%      20.00%   -1.25%   :
: Resale                    8.000      3.33%       3.00%    0.33%   :
: Service labor            15.000      6.25%       6.00%    0.25%   :
:   [ ._____]        [_____]   [_____] [_____] [_____] :
:   [_____]       [_____]   [_____] [_____] [_____] :
:                                                                  :
: Totals -->               240.000    100.00%    100.00%    .00%   :
:------------------------------------------------------------------:
```

Figure 10–1 Sales breakdown worksheet.

— 163 —

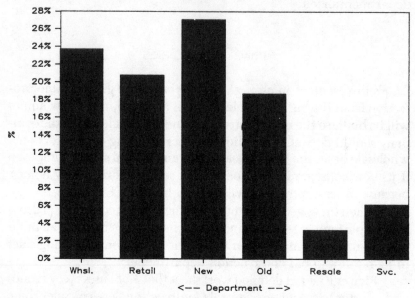

Figure 10-2 Percentage of sales column chart.

As with many lists of information, these numbers are easier to understand in the form of a picture.

Figure 10-2 plots the six areas of Central Construction Services and their percentages of total sales. It's obvious that new construction contributes the most to sales and resale the least. Kohl is generally happy with this chart, as the four major areas of the business—wholesale, retail, new construction, and old construction—all provide about the same percentage of sales. That means the company has a wide base to work from, and when one area drops, the slack should be picked up somewhere else.

Watching for Changes

The company also plots the variances in its sales to determine the deviation from the business's historical average. Often these variation lines are more useful than the raw data, as they trace how the company has changed over the period under study.

Figure 10-3 plots the variances for each department of Kohl's business. New construction has provided considerably more of the

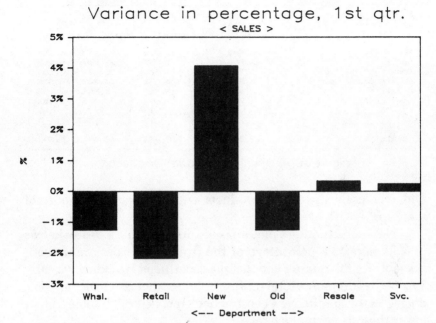

Figure 10-3 Column chart showing variance in percentage of sales.

company's total sales volume for this quarter than it usually does, and in fact the only other places with higher sales as a percentage of total sales are the company's two minor sections—resale and service. The other major departments produced sales at a lower rate than usual.

Since this data is listed on a percentage basis, when one area rises, another has to fall, so perhaps this shouldn't be a disturbing picture. Kohl is concerned, however, as wholesale sales and new construction usually rise or fall at about the same rate. Why hasn't this happened during this quarter?

Kohl continues the examination by looking at two other critical areas of the company. Most things start with sales but end at the bottom line, with profit, so that's where he looks next.

Figure 10–4 is the same worksheet that Central Construction Services used for its sales information, but this time it lists each area's profit before taxes. The time period remains the same, the first quarter of the year.

Wholesale's profits are up 6.25% in spite of lower sales. Kohl therefore examines what the department sold during the quarter, since whatever it was selling made more money for the company.

```
!-----------------------------------------------------------------!
! Profit breakdown           Total profit:      19.200            !
! 1st quarter                                                     !
!                        Amount    Percentage   Normal   Variance !
!                                                                 !
! Wholesale               6.000      31.25%     25.00%    6.25%   !
! Retail                  6.000      31.25%     23.00%    8.25%   !
! Construction (new)      1.900       9.90%     23.00% -13.10%   !
! Construction (old bldgs.) 4.000     20.83%     20.00%    0.83%   !
! Resale                    600       3.13%      3.00%    0.13%   !
! Service labor             700       3.65%      6.00%   -2.35%   !
! [            ]        [      ]    [      ]   [      ] [      ]   !
! [            ]        [      ]    [      ]   [      ] [      ]   !
!                                                                 !
! Totals -->             19,200     100.00%    100.00%    .00%    !
!-----------------------------------------------------------------!
```

Figure 10-4   Profit breakdown worksheet.

Did wholesale distribute products with a higher-than-normal markup?

New construction's picture is disturbing. Kohl already knows that its sales as a percentage of the firm's total sales are up considerably for this quarter and that the department is producing nearly 10% of the company's total profits. But these increased sales are producing less of a profit: New construction's rate of profit is some 13.10% lower than its normal average.

There's another part to this story that Kohl hasn't seen yet, though, and that's how much each part of the company contributes to gross profit. That's where Kohl looks next.

Figure 10–5 details, using the same basic format, the gross profit of each section of Central Construction Services. It shows that the only two areas that have increased are new construction (almost 7% above average) and service labor (up about .5%).

This completes the picture for Central Construction for the first quarter of the year, but what does this picture really say? Kohl knows that if the new construction department's gross profit is higher, then its direct costs have to be the same or lower, on a percentage basis,

```
!-----------------------------------------------------------------!
! Gross Profit breakdown      Total gross profit:   77.000        !
! 1st quarter                                                     !
!                        Amount    Percentage   Normal   Variance !
!                                                                 !
! Wholesale              18.000      23.38%     25.00%   -1.62%   !
! Retail                 15.000      19.48%     23.00%   -3.52%   !
! Construction (new)     23.000      29.87%     23.00%    6.87%   !
! Construction (old bldgs.) 14.000    18.18%     20.00%   -1.82%   !
! Resale                  2.000       2.60%      3.00%   -0.40%   !
! Service labor           5.000       6.49%      6.00%    0.49%   !
! [            ]        [      ]    [      ]   [      ] [      ]   !
! [            ]        [      ]    [      ]   [      ] [      ]   !
!                                                                 !
! Totals -->             77,000     100.00%    100.00%    .00%    !
!-----------------------------------------------------------------!
```

Figure 10-5   Gross profit breakdown worksheet.

```
!----------------------------------------------------------------------!
! Profit breakdown                                                     !
! 1st quarter                                     Profit               !
!                              Sales    Profit Percentage Normal Variance !
!                                                                      !
! Wholesale                   57,000    6,000     10.53%   11.00%  -0.47% !
! Retail                      50,000    6,000     12.00%   10.00%   2.00% !
! Construction (new)          65,000    1,900      2.92%    5.00%  -2.08% !
! Construction (old bldgs.)   45,000    4,000      8.89%    9.50%  -0.61% !
! Resale                       8,000      600      7.50%    7.00%   0.50% !
! Service labor               15,000      700      4.67%    5.00%  -0.33% !
! [_____]              [_____][_____] [_____] [_____][_____] !
! [_____]              [_____][_____] [_____] [_____][_____] !
!                                                                      !
' Totals -->                 240,000   19,200     8.00%    7.92%   0.08% !
!                                               (average) (average)     !
!----------------------------------------------------------------------!
```

Figure 10–6 Profit breakdown worksheet.

than they usually are. So that isn't where the problem is. If net profit is lower, then the problem must be with overhead, since nothing else can change the bottom line. Now Kohl knows what area he must examine to find and correct the problem with this department.

But what if Kohl looks at the details of the new construction department and finds there's really no way to cut its overhead? Perhaps just to estimate the cost of building new homes requires a large and expensive office staff. Possibly it's the nature of the work that overhead is simply higher than in other areas of Kohl's company. Or perhaps the new construction work leads to other work for the business, so a lower rate of profit is acceptable.

Kohl can examine two other things. The data Kohl has seen so far didn't compare each department's profit with its sales. How does new construction's profit during the period compare with its usual rate?

Figure 10–6 combines the sales information from Figure 10–1 with the profit data from Figure 10–4. Kohl can see that the new construction department has historically produced the lowest rate of profit—some 5%, on average. For the quarter shown, the net profit situation is even worse, with profits at slightly less than 3%. By comparing the department's profit with its sales, Kohl learns that it's operating at a 2.92% rate of profit.

Catch-22: Highest Sales, Lowest Profit

Central Construction Services finds itself in something of a quandary. The one department that's recording the highest sales, as a percentage of total sales, is also recording the lowest profit, both in comparison to the other departments and in terms of its own historical average. Even at that, the business as a whole for the first quarter of the year has produced about the same profit as a percentage of sales as it usually does (it's only .8% lower than normal). That means the other areas of the business are picking up the slack that exists in the new construction area.

To further explore this wide variation, Kohl took data from all the worksheets and combined it into one.

Figure 10–7 plots three data sets for the new construction department. The first is for its sales as a percentage of total sales, about 27%. The second column, the highest on the chart, plots the department's gross profit as a percentage of total gross profit, or about 30%. The lowest column, for net profit, is calculated as the percentage of profit made in relation to sales. This figure isn't calculated as a percentage of total profit (as was the data in Figure 10–4) but in relation to the sales made by the new construction department itself. On sales of some $65,000, new construction made a profit of only $1,900, or some 2.92%.

To many business owners, it might seem logical to reduce the investment in new construction since it is producing much worse

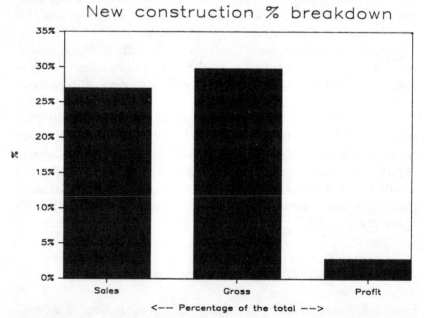

Figure 10–7 Column chart showing new construction percentage breakdown.

```
!-----------------------------------------------------------------!
!  Current                            !  With new construction     !
!                                     !  Eliminated                !
!                                     !                            !
!                 Dollar              !                 Dollar     !
!                 Volume      %       !                 Volume    %!
!                                     !                            !
!  Total sales:   240,000             !  Total sales:   175,000    !
!                                     !                            !
!  Direct costs:  163,000 67.92%      !  Direct costs:  121,000 69.14% !
!  Gross profit:   77,000 32.08%      !  Gross profit:   54,000 30.86% !
!  Overhead        57,800 24.08%      !  Overhead        57,800 33.03% !
!                                     !                            !
!  Net profit                         !  Net profit                !
!  before taxes:   19,200  8.00%      !  before taxes:  (3,800)-2.17% !
!-----------------------------------------------------------------!
```

Figure 10–8 Worksheet showing net profit with and without new construction.

profits than the other areas of the company. Others would eliminate new construction entirely and concentrate on the other, more profitable areas. Does that make sense?

To get a line on whether eliminating the department is feasible, Kohl created a new worksheet.

Figure 10–8 details two different scenarios for Central Construction Services. The left side of the worksheet shows the current situation, with the business making an 8% before-tax profit. If Kohl eliminated the new construction department, as outlined on the right side of the worksheet, the company would find itself with a $3,800 loss.

This information confirms that the problem is with the overhead of the business, as the other cost figures don't look out of line. Direct costs, for example, would rise only from about 68% of sales to 69% if the new construction division was eliminated. Gross profit would fall only about 1%. This illustration assumes that overhead will not be reduced, so it rises, as a percentage of sales, from 24% to 33%.

Naturally, if this department were eliminated, its associated overhead would decrease. The worksheet tells Kohl *how much* overhead would have to drop for the elimination to make sense. In this case, it's the amount of the recorded loss, $3,800, plus the profits the business recorded: $19,200. If the business could reduce its overhead by the sum of the two—$23,000—it would end up in the same place as it was before the new construction department was eliminated. In other words, if the overhead for the new construction division was about $23,000 a year, the department could be eliminated without hurting the company's profit level.

In this case, that isn't the situation. Kohl works backward to calculate the direct costs for the new construction department:

Sales for the department $65,000
minus gross profit   − 23,000
Direct costs $42,000

Here are all the figures for the new construction department:

		Percentage of sales
Sales	$65,000	
Direct costs	42,000	64.6%
Gross profit	23,000	35.4%
Net profit	1,900	2.9%
Overhead	$21,100	32.5%

The overhead for the new construction department, $21,110, is awfully close to the $23,000 Kohl needs to completely close it down.

If the business kept its records properly, Kohl would have the exact overhead figure for the department. This illustration shows you another way to calculate that figure in case the precise details aren't available. It's like a puzzle: If you have all but one of the pieces, you can still figure out the missing number.

You probably wouldn't want to actually eliminate an entire department but to figure out a way to greatly reduce its overhead. The CCS case study is meant to emphasize the importance of understanding where your sales and costs come from. Unless you know that, you have no control over your future.

Warning Signs

How can you tell when a segment of your business—whether a department or a type of customer—is going bad? Is there some way to determine when it's time to get out of a specific area and concentrate elsewhere?

It's not as difficult as it may sound, and the key is to do just what Kohl ended up doing: looking at the gross profit contribution of each section of your company. Often it's helpful to a company to stay in a line of work that doesn't contribute any net profit as long as it adds substantially to the gross profit. That helps pay the overhead for all parts of a company.

In my own business, as with Central Construction Services, new construction is always the worst area from the standpoint of net profit. Sadly, that's true for most companies in the construction trade, all the way from general contractors to subcontractors like electricians, plumbers, carpenters, and so on. The percentage of net profit is historically the lowest for new construction work, probably because it's so competitive. But most of us can't afford *not* to do new construction, as the large sales volume contributes so much to paying our overhead.

Usually what happens when a certain area of your work starts to get into difficulties is that it will first show decreased profits. The problem with judging from a profit standpoint only is that profits can swing wildly with only minor changes in total sales, direct material costs, and/or direct labor.

Gross profit, on the other hand, is much less influenced in terms of percentages, as it's always a much larger figure. It also isn't affected by overhead, so it's a direct measurement of how well each department or area of your business is performing in terms of sales and costs. Your direct costs come out of the total as gross profit is calculated, so they're the only things (along with sales) that get you to your gross profit figure.

Tips and Guidelines

If you sell to various kinds of customers, try to break down your sales totals to learn how much each type contributes to your business. You might find that customers you've sold to before make the most profit for your business, while new customers expect more in the way of service, shop around more, and so on. That would tell you not only that you make more money when you make a second or third sale to someone but also that you might be able to raise your markup to existing customers. They're not as likely to comparison-shop. Each new customer costs dollars in advertising and sales time; each existing, happy customer costs next to nothing.

Along this same line, take a look at the cost of getting prospects into your store in relation to the sales they bring in. Central Construction Services did this for its new construction department and found it had made estimates, over the past year, to 45 prospects. Out of those potential customers, six contracted for new homes, for a sales volume of $280,000 (the quarter that Kohl examined in detail recorded $65,000 of this total).

Here's what the company spent on advertising for these prospects:

Newspaper advertising	$3,200
Radio advertising	600
Yellow Pages advertising	4,700
Direct mail	800
	$9,400

There's no way to judge from these figures if the money was wisely spent, but you can tell that for each of the 45 people who brought in his or her new home plans for an estimate, the company spent $210 ($9,400 ÷ 45 prospects = $210 each).

If you do this same breakdown for your own business, you might be surprised by the result, for it will usually be higher than you expect. You'll also gain an appreciation for your potential customers, as you'll know what it costs you just for a chance to talk to them.

How else can you break down your customer/product mix? If you can't do it by specific department or by type of customer, take a look at it by seasons of the year. Most businesses are very seasonal— more than they would like to be. The air-conditioning business that booms during the summer may die on the vine around Christmas. The plumbing business that records all kinds of sales during the spring and summer may have a hard time once the ground becomes frozen during fall. The specialty shop may record more than half its business in the period between Thanksgiving and Christmas and starve the rest of the year. It makes sense for a seasonal business to increase its markup when times are good and lower it when things get a little slow.

Also consider what other products might interest your existing customers. Start a simple file that notes what you sold and what else a customer might purchase from you. From time to time, send the customer some literature or call if anything new comes up. Most people want to own the newest, the latest model of whatever you sell; sometimes you just have to let your customers know about it and you've made a sale.

11

How to Build a *Thinking* Budget Your Banker Will Love

Since most everyone would agree that many business failures are caused by a lack of financial planning and control, it's hard to understand why every business owner doesn't do a better job when it comes to planning and budgeting. Well, perhaps not so hard: Budgeting is painstaking work that all too often ends up being so far off the mark that it hardly seems worth the trouble. That's because many business owners have the notion that their budgets are written in stone, though it's completely wrong to assume that even budgeted figures cannot change.

If somehow you can forecast accurately even just a few of your business's financial details, you'll come up with a good budget that will give you all sorts of information about your business future. You'll know in advance about your:

- Sales
    - by month
    - by quarter
    - one period compared with another
- Direct costs
- Overhead
- Gross profit

- Net profit
    in dollars and as a percentage of sales
    one period compared with another
- Expected cash inflow
- Anticipated cash requirements
    when to expect the cash and/or when you'll need to borrow

In addition to preparing accurate forecasts and using current data to update projected figures, you should always make logical comparisons between past information and current figures. When there's a deviation in the numbers, it's important to determine why it has occurred. And you should take things a step further and examine the cause/effect relationship that exists between many of the slices of your financial pie.

Budget Variations: Your Estimated and Actual Figures

Let's consider the WoodShop, a small company that usually has eight employees, who spend their time producing bookshelves, kitchen cabinets, and the like for both custom installations and for tract homes. John, the owner of the WoodShop, does all the estimating and sales work. He has a wide range of customers, including individual homeowners and building contractors.

John watches for variations in his budget, and let's say he finds one in the advertising account. For the past six months, the WoodShop has spent more on advertising than he had anticipated. To determine why actual costs were higher, John checks to see if he ran a major promotion that will have an impact on sales at a later date (meaning that the total cost of the promotion shouldn't be charged to the current period). He makes sure that any increase in ad rates has been factored into his budgeted figures. He determines if he's advertising in more media than originally planned. (Often it's easy to say yes to an advertising salesperson without checking the budget to see if the dollars to pay for the advertising really exist). John also needs to make sure he received all the co-op advertising money that's available to his business and helps to cut the total cost.

There is always a reason that actual costs deviate from estimated expenditures. You might find, as another example, that your direct costs have unexpectedly decreased as a percentage of sales, perhaps because your labor costs are lower than what you anticipated. In the WoodShop's case, John might learn that the two people who glue the cabinets are using a different technique. Or perhaps they're stacking the cabinets differently, which makes production go more smoothly, or working together more effectively than some of his other employees. John may learn that his business is producing more of a specific type of cabinet that has lower costs during this time but will have higher costs over the next six months.

John must also consider where any changes in the WoodShop's figures take place. Advertising is an overhead item, which means it won't vary according to sales, so John can make a direct comparison between what he spent last year and what he's currently spending. Direct labor, on the other hand, should vary in direct proportion to John's sales: On average, direct labor should stay at about the same percentage of sales figure. What this means is that John wants to examine advertising both as a dollar figure and as a percentage of his sales (and perhaps also as a percentage of his overhead).

Cost Relationships

Let's say you hire a new, two-person installation crew at a total hourly cost of $32, including associated taxes and insurance costs. Each day, then, your direct costs (not including the materials this crew will install) will increase by $256; your weekly direct costs will increase by $1,280. If your standard markup is 30%, then you would divide your direct costs of $1,280 by .70, which tells you your weekly sales should increase by $1,829.

After just a few weeks, you should be able to tell exactly if this crew is paying its own way. If your sales don't come up to expectations, you need to determine why this crew isn't pulling its weight. Have the jobs it's worked on been more complex than usual? Are the people in the crew still learning how to work together? Comparing your estimated and actual time and dollar costs will help you pinpoint the crew's problems.

This same line of reasoning can be applied to individual employees to evaluate their performance. Sales should increase for their exact cost with its markup, plus the retail value of any materials they sell.

Budget Comparisons

The first step is to create some kind of comparison that's easy and informative. Figure 11–1 is a worksheet you can use for each budget category with spaces for each individual line item within that category. The worksheet can cover any period you like; it can be monthly, quarterly, semiannual, or yearly. Start with the estimated

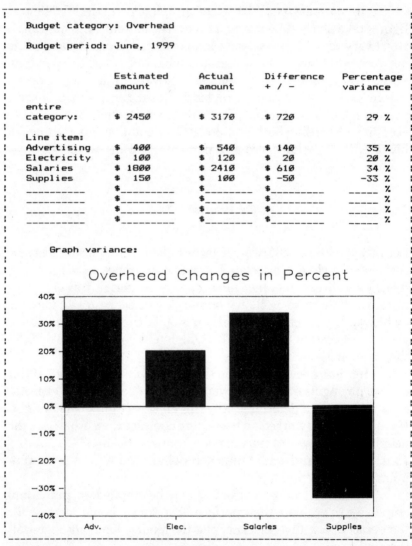

Figure 11–1 Worksheet and column chart showing budget variance.

and actual totals for the entire category and list any variances in dollars or percentages. To enter overhead amounts, start with your total actual and estimated costs for each category, then fill in each line item (advertising, telephone bills, utilities, and so on).

The percentage variance line tells you when things are getting better or worse. Since it's usually easier to see a variance when it's plotted as a percentage, there's a space on the bottom of the worksheet for a column graph. The line items are entered here only when they show a variance that you might find useful to chart, such as a change in your overhead expenses (in this example, you spent more than you had budgeted for advertising, electricity, and office salaries and less than expected for office supplies).

The percentage deviation scale on the left side of the graph can be adjusted to fit any individual business's requirements.

Keeping a Running Budget

Usually a business creates a budget at the end of the year that estimates what will happen over the next 12 months. The owner then compares the company's actual results with the forecasted ones as the year goes on. But I'd like to suggest that you keep what can be called a *running budget*. In December you plan for the January/December period; in January plan for the February/January period, and so on. This gives you an ongoing idea of what you can expect from your business during each month.

One of the best things about a running budget is that it keeps your budgeting up-to-date with the latest financial data. And when December comes along, you'll have to update only one month's projected cost and sales data, and you'll be done for your standard next-year forecast. It's easier to budget a month at a time, rather than trying to handle the whole worksheet in one sitting.

Your Banker's Budget

It probably won't come as a major surprise to any business owner that the financial data a banker looks at aren't necessarily the same figures the business owner pays attention to.

A bank will want to examine a business's budget before it approves almost any loan, particularly if the company is young. First, the banker wants to know if the owner's projections for the company seem reasonable and in keeping with the financial details of the business. Second, the banker wants to know where the loan funds will be applied and where the dollars will come from to repay them. For example, you may need to borrow cash to pay for purchases of equipment and material for a big job you have coming up. As the work progresses, you'll use the funds you've been paid to take care of the loan. If your situation is more complex—say, you have a number of upcoming jobs that will require at least partial financing—a detailed budget will make it easier for your banker to understand and justify your loan. If you require funding for a number of projects with various time frames, include each project with its own budget line and indicate when you'll need the money and when you expect to pay it back. That helps the bank appreciate that you know what you're doing with its money.

Your budget should be accurate enough to truly look into the company's future, reflecting the trends and pitfalls of the business you're in.

A workable, logical budget gives the banker a sense of security. If you have a problem repaying your loan, he can use the copy of your budget in his files to justify his approval of your loan.

Finally, devising a budget for the bank makes you examine your figures in a more critical light. All too often, it's easy to accept things without checking them completely, and looking at your numbers as an outsider would forces you to think a little harder about your data.

Your Budget as a Working Tool

The budget you present to your bank must be in a format that your banker can use and is familiar with. If you don't put the data into the right form, the bank will categorize them as it sees fit, and often that means your numbers are misinterpreted.

It's important to remember that every business has its own way of operating and of keeping records. For example, you may own the building your business uses. If you want to give yourself a raise, it might make sense from a tax standpoint to pay yourself a higher rent on the property you lease to the company rather than increasing your salary. But that skews your books; a loan officer will look at those figures and wonder why the rent you pay is higher than what your peers are paying. Or perhaps you want to give yourself a larger salary to avoid paying what amounts to a double tax if your company declared and paid dividends (the business is taxed on what it earns, and then you're taxed on the dividend income you receive from it). But a banker might examine those numbers and wonder why your salary is so high in comparison to what others in your own industry pay their officers. Perhaps you just purchased a piece of equipment that's going to make your business more productive, and decided, because of good budget projections and your tax situation, to make larger payments than you normally would. That will make what you're spending on the current portion of your long-term debt higher than what it should be and higher than what others in your industry report. Again, unless you break it out, your banker will wonder (and worry) why your company's figures are off the norm.

You've either got to explain each of your unique business details to your banker or put the data in a form that makes it easy for him to figure them out. So you need to use the same categories your banker will examine, usually those found in Robert Morris Associates' *Annual Statement Studies*.

Your banker will usually compare your data with that of others in your local area. Let's remember that the bank is also loaning money to your competition and knows their sales, profits, overhead, salaries, and so on.

Most banks have a form they use for a business loan application, so that the company's financial data is arranged in a standard format. Ask your banker for a copy and use it to give the bank your data, rather than having them fill out the form for you. Their categories are usually a bit different from the ones you use; your accounting system, after all, was designed to fit your individual business, whereas the bank must use standardized forms or they won't be able to compare your company with others.

The Importance of Accuracy

When you prepare the budget you'll give your banker, you have to take special care to make sure the numbers are accurate. If there's anything that's not correct, the bank will almost always spot it, then question your other figures.

Let's consider an abbreviated budget worksheet for the Wood-Shop and how a banker might examine it. John starts with sales to determine if his projected sales figures are in line with what he really expected to record. If his sales are seasonal, he should indicate this to his banker.

Where else will John get cash from? If he allows people to charge at least part of their purchases through an accounts receivable system, then some of the dollars he collects (which will help John service any outstanding loans) will come from the payments people make on what they owe. If John shows this expected cash inflow in his budget, he'll want to provide a list of who, by name, owes the Wood-Shop what and how old those accounts are. It's probably worthwhile to eliminate those accounts over 90 days old, as they may not be collectible. Although your figures will look a bit worse, they will be more accurate.

The list also indicates the diversity of your accounts receivable amounts. It's almost always better to have 1,000 people who each owe you $1, rather than one person who owes you $1,000. Sometimes businesses get into quick trouble by having all their accounts receivable in too few accounts, putting them at great risk—if one major customer has problems.

Cash Flow Projection

Naturally, you want your forecasted budget to show an accurate cash flow projection, so it's important to keep in mind that cash flow is profit plus depreciation *less* any increases in assets. Many business owners were brought up believing that cash flow is recorded profit plus depreciation, but from a banker's viewpoint, that's not correct. For example, if your business shows an expected profit for an upcoming quarter of, say, $20,000 and asset increases of $15,000 during that same period (assets include, of course, current assets such as inventory and accounts receivable), the business has only $5,000 to handle its debts. If it already has debt service of about that amount, it won't have the ability to increase its accounts receivable or inventory or any of its fixed asset accounts (buildings, trucks, equipment). What if sales really start to boom? The business probably won't be able to take advantage of any possible increase, as it won't have any additional cash. A loan officer will deduce that the company also won't be able to increase its debt service.

Consider combining some of the cost line items on your budget so they match the categories your banker works with. The major categories—gross profit, overhead, net profit—should also show percentages based on sales volume. Break your budget down by quarters too, as larger totals often make a problem easier to spot.

Figure 11–2, an abbreviated budget for the WoodShop, isn't as detailed a worksheet as the company might use internally, but rather it's the kind of budget it would give its banker. While your internal budget should match the reporting categories used by your accounting system, the one you produce for outside distribution should be as standard as possible. For example, you might break down your office expenses into postage, office salaries, paperwork and supplies, copy machine costs, and so on, but if you're making a budget for external use you should combine them into one office expense account.

The major areas in the worksheet designed for the WoodShop's bank, shown as Figure 11–2, are the same ones listed in the *Annual Statement Studies*. The banker has already calculated the percentages for each category, as that makes it easier to see changes as they occur. It's almost always worthwhile to graph this information, on both a dollar and on a percentage basis, as a picture is often more understandable than the raw data itself.

Figure 11–3 holds quarterly summary data from the WoodShop's monthly budget worksheet. These larger figures, presented in the same format as the monthly data, are often easier to understand, as they show more of the forest and fewer of the trees.

In this case, John's concerned about the third quarter, which had the highest profit before taxes of any of the periods. Is that quarter always better than any other? Why? If these figures are correct, John should attach a little note to this budget explaining why the third quarter will be his best and also documenting why it has been so in past years. He might also explain why the WoodShop's sales and profits are worst during the second quarter.

If your budget is like most others, something always seems to come along during the year to gum up the whole thing. Oh, the initial forecasts were pretty good, and for a time perhaps the actual results for sales and costs stayed close to what you expected them to be, but as the year wore on, things just *happened* that made your initial budget end up way off its mark. That's because most budgets don't take into account how things change over time. Budgets must be examined and revised as the year progresses.

What you want to do is to create a budget grid that combines and compares your estimated data with your actual amounts. For

Budget worksheet	JAN	% of sales	FEB	% of sales	MAR	% of sales	APR	% of sales	//	NOV	% of sales	DEC	% of sales
Monthly sales	50,000		55,000		60,000		50,000		//	62,000		65,000	
Cumulative sales	50,000		105,000		165,000		215,000		//	590,000		655,000	
Direct cost items:									//				
Direct Labor costs	12,000	24%	14,000	24%	12,500	25%	12,000	21%	//	13,000	21%	13,000	20%
Material costs	25,000	50%	23,000	50%	26,500	42%	25,000	44%	//	26,000	42%	28,000	43%
Total direct costs	37,000	74%	37,000	74%	39,000	67%	37,000	65%	//	39,000	63%	41,000	63%
Gross profit	13,000	26%	18,000	26%	21,000	33%	13,000	35%	//	23,000	37%	24,000	37%
Overhead items:									//				
Office payroll	3,000	6%	3,500	6%	4,000	6%	3,000	7%	//	3,500	6%	3,000	5%
Other overhead	7,000	14%	7,500	14%	7,500	14%	7,000	13%	//	7,500	12%	7,000	11%
Total overhead	10,000	20%	11,000	20%	11,500	20%	10,000	19%	//	11,000	18%	10,000	15%
Total costs	47,000	94%	48,000	94%	50,500	87%	47,000	84%	//	61,000	98%	61,000	94%
Cumulative costs	47,000		95,000		145,500		47,001		//	520,776		581,776	
Starting profit (before taxes)	0		3,000		10,000		19,500		//	77,000		78,000	
Monthly profit (before taxes)	3,000	6%	7,000	6%	9,500	13%	3,000	16%	//	1,000	2%	4,000	6%
Cumulative profit (before taxes)	3,000	6%	10,000	6%	19,500	10%	22,500	12%	//	78,000	13%	82,000	13%

Figure 11-2 Budget worksheet for January–December.

Budget worksheet	First Quarter Quarterly Totals	% of sales	Second Quarter Quarterly Totals	% of sales	Third Quarter Quarterly Totals	% of sales	Fourth Quarter Quarterly Totals	% of sales	Year-to-date Yearly Totals	% of sales
Quarterly sales	165,000		155,000		175,000		160,000		655,000	
Direct cost items:										
Direct Labor costs	38,500	23.33%	37,000	23.87%	42,000	24.00%	37,000	23.13%	154,501	23.59%
Material costs	74,500	45.15%	75,000	48.39%	82,000	46.86%	75,000	46.88%	306,502	46.79%
Total direct costs	113,000	68.48%	112,000	72.26%	124,000	70.86%	112,000	70.00%	461,003	70.38%
Gross profit	52,000	31.52%	43,000	27.74%	51,000	29.14%	48,000	30.00%	194,001	29.62%
Overhead items:										
Office payroll	10,500	6.36%	11,000	7.10%	11,000	6.29%	11,000	6.88%	43,500	6.64%
Other overhead	22,000	13.33%	21,000	13.55%	21,000	12.00%	21,000	13.13%	85,001	12.98%
Total overhead	32,500	19.70%	32,000	20.65%	32,000	18.29%	32,000	20.00%	128,501	19.62%
Total costs										
Cumulative costs	145,500	88.18%	147,000	94.84%	147,000	84.00%	147,000	91.88%	586,504	89.54%
Starting profit	19,500		19,500		27,500		55,500		68,500	
Quarterly profit	19,500	11.82%	8,000		28,000		13,000		68,496	
Cumulative profit (before taxes)			27,500	5.16%	55,500	16.00%	68,500	8.13%	136,996	10.46%

Figure 11–3 Budget worksheet, showing quarters in boxes.

instance, if your sales increase 5% during the first month of the year, your grid will reflect the rise and show the sales figures for the rest of the months of the year also increasing at 5% per month. If your direct material costs drop 2.1%, your grid will reflect this decrease in its projected direct material cost figures.

Note that none of this eliminates your original estimated figures; instead, you're adding a new grid with a space for each revenue and cost line item, where you will fill in the numbers based on your new forecast.

Most budgets are done on columnar sheets, with one column for each month and a row for each line item. To make things easy, let's label the columns that run left to right across the page with letters and the rows that run up and down the page with numbers. You'll end up with this basic design:

	←Columns→					
	A	B	C	~	AA	AB
Row 1→						
Row 2→						
~						
Row 50→						
Row 51→						

The place where a column and row intersect is called a *cell*. Cell B15, for example, is the spot where column B intersects with row 15.

Normally, you use the columns to represent the passage of time (in a budget, usually each month gets its own column), and the rows hold the different categories (overhead, sales for each department, etc.). I suggest is that you add a section to your current columnar budget for a new grid in which you'll enter projected figures. Your worksheet might end up like this:

Columns A–N estimated data	Columns P–AB actual data	Columns AD–AO projected data

Early in the year your projected figures are not going to be as accurate as they will be when more months have passed and you have more data on which to base your projections. If sales are up 5% after one month, for example, it doesn't necessarily mean that they will rise 5% each month for the remainder of the year. But as you progress month by month through the year, you'll average these percentage increases and decreases, so your projected figures will be more refined and accurate.

Whenever you start your budgeting process for the next year, you begin by making an educated guess about each amount for every month much as John did for his categories, as shown in Figure 11–4. To keep his worksheet as easy to read as possible, John lumped the budget categories together, so he has only two overhead breakdowns, two direct cost items, and so on.

You might start by putting categories together to make large units (sales, direct costs, overhead) until you're familiar with the process and the math involved. Then you can split out the details that are the most useful to your company.

John's sample budget assumes the business collects for everything it sells, at least from a profit standpoint. In the real world, that's seldom the case, but most businesses operate on the accrual method of accounting, which means sales and costs are recorded in the month the sales are made and costs incurred, whether the business gets paid for the sales and/or pays its bills during that month or not.

John used figures that will make the percentage increases in his projected budget easy to see. For the first half of the year, in Figure 11–4, all of his monthly sales are estimated at $50,000, and all costs are identical for each month. In real life, monthly sales and cost line items (even estimated ones) are never the same, as the expected figures are based on historical averages as well as on an educated guess. However, using these rounded figures as base monthly amounts makes it easier to see the dollar changes that occur.

During the second half of the year in Figure 11–4—the months of July through December—John's budget looks more like what a real budget looks like, with more exact estimates of sales, costs, and so on.

As the new year comes along and John starts to record data for those months, he'll have something like Figure 11–5. Here, data for the first six months of the year have been put into place. Sales for January were a bit more than anticipated (the $52,100 in cell Q4 instead of the expected $50,000), while costs were a bit higher too ($47,792 instead of $47,000). John's cash inflow, then, is slightly more than what he thought it would be ($4,308 instead of $3,000).

February's sales are better, and its profit before taxes is slightly higher than January's actual results. March came in with sales a bit

These figures are rounded-off, as that makes it easier to see the percentage changes in our projected budget.

These figures are more exact estimates, based on past business history, so they give us a better idea of real sales and cost figures.

	A	B	C JAN	D FEB	E MAR	F APR	G MAY	H JUN	I JUL	J AUG	K SEP	L OCT	M NOV	N DEC
1	Budget worksheet													
2														
3			(Estimated at the beginning of the year)											
4	Monthly sales -->		50,000	50,000	50,000	50,000	50,000	50,000	53,000	55,000	55,000	60,000	62,000	65,000
5	Cumulative sales -->		50,000	100,000	150,000	200,000	250,000	300,000	353,000	408,000	463,000	523,000	585,000	650,000
6														
7														
8	Overhead items:													
9	Office payroll		3,000	3,000	3,000	3,000	3,000	3,000	3,000	3,000	3,000	3,000	3,000	3,000
10	Other overhead		7,000	7,000	7,000	7,000	7,000	7,000	7,000	7,000	7,000	7,000	7,000	7,000
11														
12	Direct cost items:													
13	Direct Labor costs		12,000	12,000	12,000	12,000	12,000	12,000	10,600	11,000	11,000	12,000	12,400	13,000
14	Material costs		25,000	25,000	25,000	25,000	25,000	25,000	27,560	28,600	28,600	31,200	32,240	33,800
15														
16	Total costs		47,000	47,000	47,000	47,000	47,000	47,000	48,160	49,600	49,600	53,200	54,640	56,800
17	Cumulative costs		47,000	94,000	141,000	188,000	235,000	282,000	330,160	379,760	429,360	482,560	537,200	594,000
18														
19	Starting profit		0	3,000	6,000	9,000	12,000	15,000	18,000	22,840	28,240	33,640	40,440	47,800
20	Monthly profit (before taxes)		3,000	3,000	3,000	3,000	3,000	3,000	4,840	5,400	5,400	6,800	7,360	8,200
21	Cumulative profit (before taxes)		3,000	6,000	9,000	12,000	15,000	18,000	22,840	28,240	33,640	40,440	47,800	56,000
22														

Figure 11-4 Budget worksheet, showing both rounded-off and exact figures.

	P	Q	R	S	T	U	V	W		
		JAN	FEB	MAR	APR	MAY	JUN	JUL	AB	DEC
1	Budget worksheet - actual data									
2										
3										
4	Monthly sales --->	52,100	53,100	50,982	45,455	43,443	56,565			
5	Cumulative sales --->	52,100	105,200	156,182	201,637	245,080	301,645			
6										
7										
8	Overhead items:									
9	Office payroll	3,180	3,200	3,100	3,000	3,100	3,000			
10	Other overhead	7,100	7,000	7,100	7,200	7,000	7,000			
11										
12	Direct cost items:									
13	Direct Labor costs	10,420	10,620	10,196	9,091	8,689	11,313			
14	Material costs	27,092	27,612	26,511	23,637	22,590	29,414			
15										
16	Total costs	47,792	48,432	46,907	42,928	41,379	50,727			
17	Cumulative costs	47,792	96,224	143,131	186,059	227,438	278,164			
18										
19	Starting profit	0	4,308	8,976	13,051	15,578	17,642			
20	Monthly profit (before taxes)	4,308	4,668	4,075	2,527	2,054	5,838			
21	Cumulative profit (before taxes)	4,308	8,976	13,051	15,578	17,642	23,481			
22										

Figure 11-5   Budget worksheet, showing actual data through June.

lower, but costs were down too. This is typical for any business with a good budgeting process—sales, cash received, and costs are close to the estimated figures.

John next takes these actual figures, averages them, and compares them with his average estimated figures, then raises or lowers the sales, costs, and cash figures for each remaining month in his new budget grid. As each actual monthly figure is recorded, John's new worksheet gets more and more accurate.

Figure 11-6 shows the end result—a new section of John's worksheet that forecasts his sales and costs. Since John can't make a projection until January's actual sales are recorded, he's filled in estimated figures based on the January figures from his original worksheet (Figure 11-4).

February's projected sales are based on two things: the sales John expects (the $50,000 in cell D4 in Figure 11-4) and the actual figure for January (the $52,100 in cell Q4 of Figure 11-5). Since sales increased $2,100 (or 4.2%), the projected budget increased February's estimated sales figure by $2,100. This amount—$52,100—is entered as projected February sales (cell AE4).

March's projected sales figure (cell AF4 in Figure 11-6) is calculated the same way, but now John has two actual sales amounts to work with, so he averages them and compares the result with to the average of the original estimated sales for the first two months of the year. With the figures in his sample worksheet, the amounts for January's actual sales ($52,100) and February's sales ($53,100) are added together and averaged. The total is compared with the average estimated sales for the first two months (in this example, of course, they average $50,000). Here, the two months of actual data average 5.2% more than the sales John originally estimated, so March's projected sales figure is $52,600 (cell AF4).

Let's go back to Figure 11-4, which shows the WoodShop's original estimates. In a real-world worksheet, the estimated sales and costs figures will be different for each month; he'll never have exactly the same sales and costs every month. For the last half of the year, John's estimated sales and cost figures are closer to what his business can expect. Instead of round numbers, he shows amounts approximating actual data, just as a real budget estimate would have.

It's easy to see, in Figure 11-6, what the formula's done with these numbers. John's total sales (and cash collected figures) are higher than estimated on his original worksheet, so the numbers for his cash balance are higher. That allows John to plan for a better

1 Budget worksheet - forecasted amounts

		AD	AE	AF	AG	AH	AI	AJ	AK	AL	AM	AN	AO
		JAN	FEB	MAR	APR	MAY	JUN	JUL	AUG	SEP	OCT	NOV	DEC
4	Monthly sales -->	50,000	52,100	52,600	52,061	50,409	49,016	50,274	52,838	49,900	54,336	58,233	59,115
5	Cumulative sales -->	50,000	102,100	154,700	206,761	257,170	306,186	356,460	409,298	459,198	513,533	571,766	630,881
6													
7													
8	Overhead items:												
9	Office payroll	3,000	3,180	3,190	3,160	3,120	3,116	3,097	3,097	3,097	3,097	3,097	3,097
10	Other overhead	7,000	7,100	7,050	7,067	7,100	7,080	7,067	7,067	7,067	7,067	7,067	7,067
11													
12	Direct cost items:												
13	Direct Labor costs	12,000	10,420	10,520	10,412	10,082	9,803	8,882	8,521	9,555	10,482	10,785	11,233
14	Material costs	25,000	27,092	27,352	27,072	26,213	25,488	28,820	26,796	29,384	31,620	32,003	32,882
15													
16	Total costs	47,000	47,792	48,112	47,710	46,515	45,488	47,865	45,481	49,103	52,265	52,952	54,278
17	Cumulative costs	47,000	94,792	142,904	190,614	237,129	282,617	330,481	375,962	425,065	477,330	530,282	584,560
18													
19	Starting profit	0	3,000	7,308	11,796	16,146	20,041	23,569	25,979	33,336	34,139	36,203	41,484
20	Monthly profit (before taxes)	3,000	4,308	4,488	4,350	3,895	3,528	2,409	7,357	797	2,071	5,281	4,837
21	Cumulative profit (before taxes)	3,000	7,308	11,796	16,146	20,041	23,569	25,979	33,336	34,133	36,203	41,484	46,321

Figure 11-6 Budget worksheet, showing forecasted amounts through December.

Worksheet to calculate forecasted dollar totals for _____

	Feb	Mar	Apr	May	//	Dec
Actual total	[.......]	[.......]	[.......]	[.......]	//	[.......]
Expected amount	[.......]	[.......]	[.......]	[.......]	//	[.......]
Number of months	2	3	4	5	//	12
Average (actual)	[.......]	[.......]	[.......]	[.......]	//	[.......]
Average (expected)	[.......]	[.......]	[.......]	[.......]	//	[.......]
Difference +/-	[.......]	[.......]	[.......]	[.......]	//	[.......]
Difference %	[.......]	[.......]	[.......]	[.......]	//	[.......]
Forecasted total for next month:	[.......]	[.......]	[.......]	[.......]	//	[.......]

Figure 11-7 Worksheet to forecast dollar totals.

year than he had expected, so he might consider additional equipment purchases, greater capital investment, and so on.

Figure 11–7 is a blank worksheet to forecast your budget figures. Use one of these worksheets for each budget line item (you'll want to lump many line items together, or you'll have too many worksheets). It starts with February, as you need at least two months of data to start the forecasting process.

Figure 11–8 shows a sample worksheet filled out for the first six months of the year (actually, because John has to start in February, there are only five months of data listed). The figures in the first two lines are cumulative amounts for actual sales (from Figure 11–5) and estimated ones (from Figure 11–4). The WoodShop recorded actual sales of $105,200 for the first two months of the year, while it had expected sales of $100,000. When those figures are divided by the number of months of data, John has an average actual sales figure of $52,600 and an estimated one of $50,000. The difference, $2,600, is shown in the next line, followed by the percentage difference of 5.2%.

The last line under the Feb column is next month's expected sales. Since his sales are up 5.2% (or .052 in decimal form) for the year so far, he expects March's sales to be up that same amount. To forecast his sales figure, he adds 1 to his percentage increase and ends up with 1.052. He then multiplies this number by his anticipated sales figure for March, or $50,000: 1.052 × 50,000 = $52,600. John enters this figure into cell AF4 of the worksheet shown in Figure 11–6.

Once you have sales, cash received, and cost figures for a month,

Worksheet to calculate forecasted dollar totals for SALES

	Feb	Mar	Apr	May	Jun	Jul		Dec
Actual total	105,200	156,182	201,637	245,080	301,645	[.......]		[.......]
Expected amount	100,000	150,000	200,000	250,000	300,000	[.......]		[.......]
Number of months	2	3	4	5	6	7		12
Average (actual)	52,600	52,061	50,409	49,016	50,274	[.......]		[.......]
Average (expected)	50,000	50,000	50,000	50,000	50,000	[.......]		[.......]
Difference +/-	2,600	2,061	409	(984)	274	[.......]		[.......]
Difference %	5.20%	4.12%	0.82%	-1.97%	0.55%	[.......]		[.......]
Forecasted total for next month:	52,600	52,061	50,409	49,016	50,274	[.......]		[.......]

Figure 11-8 Worksheet to calculate forecasted dollar totals. Sales details are filled in.

use the worksheets shown in Figures 11–7/11–8 to calculate your projected amounts. These figures are then entered into the forecast grid that's shown in Figure 11–6. Forecast each month's figures using your actual and estimated totals for the preceding month.

Keep in mind that you want to use cumulative figures, which are then divided by the number of months so far in the year. Here are the cells that you'll refer to for the first few months of the year:

Month→	February	March	April	May
Cells for estimated data→ (from Figure 11–4)	C4	C4, D4	C4, D4, E4	C4, D4, E4, F4
Cells for actual data→ (from Figure 11–5)	Q4	Q4, R4	Q4, R4, S4	Q4, R4, S4, T4

This budget, combining your projected and estimated figures, is an excellent management tool.

Tips and Guidelines

A budget is often a useful device to give to your suppliers. Since they often have more invested in your company than your bank does, they sometimes have more of an interest in your financial well-being.

Design your budgets as crisis-avoidance tools that highlight when you'll have cash problems so you can prevent them from happening. After all, that's one thing a workable budget will display— when you'll need cash.

If you're thinking about opening another store or relocating, plug all your expected sales and cost figures into your budget worksheets. They will show not only when you might need to borrow money but also where the funds to pay the loans will come from and when they will come.

Try not to make any financial decisions without consulting your budget. Even something as small as a change in your advertising can throw things off. Remember, it's always worthwhile to consider the impact of a proposed expense before you sign the contract or write the check.

Glossary

Accounting: The process of recording and summarizing the financial transactions of a business.

Accounting period: A period of time during which a company's financial statements will detail the transactions it recorded; often one year. This is the span of time an income statement covers.

Accounts payable: What a company owes its suppliers for products and/or services it has purchased from them for resale, as well as what it owes for operating expenses. Suppliers must be paid within the next year or operating cycle (and usually much sooner), so accounts payable are part of the business's current liabilities. They're also called *trade payables*.

Accounts receivable: What customers owe for goods or services; essentially, loans made to customers. Usually, not all of these customers pay their bills, so most financial statements show an allowance for bad debts deducted from total receivables.

Accounts receivable turnover: A figure representing the number of times during a year that the average amount of a company's accounts receivable are collected. To calculate this figure, divide net credit sales for the year—those sales that customers are allowed to charge through an accounts receivable system—by the average net accounts receivable amount.

Accrual basis of accounting: An accounting method that records revenue in the period during which it is earned and expenses for the period during which they are incurred whether or not the company collects for the sale and/or pays for the expenses during the same period. Compare with *cash basis of accounting*.

Accumulated depreciation: A measure of the portion of the cost of an asset that has been depreciated since the asset was purchased.

Acid-test ratio: Also called the quick ratio, divides *quick assets* (cash, marketable securities, and net accounts receivable) by current liabilities. Inventories and any prepaid expenses are not considered quick assets because they might not be converted into cash within the accounting period.

Aging of accounts receivable: A listing that shows, in detail or in summary form, the age of a business's accounts receivable. Generally, the older an account gets, the greater the chance that it will not be paid and the less it's worth.

Amortization: The regular allocation of the cost of intangible assets to the periods benefiting from their use.

Annual report: A detailed record, covering a specific period of time, of the financial transactions of a business. It includes the income statement and balance sheet.

Assets: Items of value; the resources of a business.

Asset turnover rate: A figure that indicates how often operating assets turn. It is calculated by dividing net sales by operating assets (those used to operate a company). The more a business earns per dollar of operating assets, the more effectively it is being managed.

Average collection period: The average number of days it takes for customers to pay for work charged through an accounts receivable system. It is calculated by dividing the number of days in the year by the accounts receivable turnover rate. Also called the *number of days in accounts receivable*, this ratio is a measure of the quality of a company's accounts receivable, and it should be close to the payment terms requested from customers.

Average payable period: The average length of time it takes a company to pay for its purchases and/or services (products bought for resale) from its suppliers, as well as its expenses. See *accounts payable*.

Bad debts: The estimated amount of accounts receivable that a business won't collect.

Balance sheet: A report that lists the assets and equities (also called liabilities and owner's equity) at a particular moment in time. It compares what assets a business owns or controls with the claims any creditors have against those assets. The difference is what the owners of the company can claim as their equity in the firm.

Beginning inventory: The amount of inventory on hand at the start of an accounting period.

Book value of an asset: The value of assets net of accumulated depreciation.

Break-even chart: A graph that shows a visual representation of a company's break-even point.

Break-even point: The sales volume at which a company neither makes a profit nor loses money; its sales revenue exactly equals its direct costs and operating expenses.

Budgeting: A business plan that predicts a company's finances during a particular period of time.

Capital: A term that describes the amount of investment the owners have made in a business (also called equity capital). When defined as *working capital*, it can also mean *funds*, or the dollars a company has to do business with.

Capital asset: Any item of property other than inventory, accounts receivable, land and building, and intangible assets.

Capital budgeting: The planning and financing of major capital expenses for a business.

Cash and cash equivalents: All cash, marketable securities, and any other assets that can be instantly converted into cash.

Cash basis of accounting: A method of accounting that records revenue and/or expenses during a period only if the item is actually collected and/or paid for during that specific period of time; contrast to the accrual method of accounting.

Cash budget: A forecast of expected cash inflow and outgo, as well as cash balance, during a specific period; a planning tool that focuses on cash flow rather than accrued items.

Cash capability: A business's total capital, comprising its available cash and any available, but not currently used, credit.

Cash flow statement: A detailed analysis of the cash collected (or expected to be collected) or disbursed during a specific period of time. The statement details the changes in a business's cash balance by summarizing the cash receipts and disbursements that took place over the accounting period.

Collection period: See *average collection period*.

Cost of goods sold: The total direct costs for material and labor that can be traced directly to the products a company sold during a specific period of time.

Current assets: Assets that are expected to be converted into cash (or are already in the form of cash) within a reasonable period, usually one year or one operating cycle. Current assets usually include inventory and accounts receivable.

Current liabilities: Obligations that the business is expected to discharge within the next year or operating cycle. These include accounts payable, as well as any notes due and payable within the next year or operating cycle.

Current maturity, long-term debt: The amount of long-term debt that must be paid within the next 12 months.

Current ratio: A measurement of a firm's ability to pay current debts from the liquidation (conversion into cash) of its current assets. It is calculated by dividing current assets by current liabilities.

Depreciable cost: The cost of a depreciable asset less any salvage value.

Depreciation: An estimate of the value of an asset that is lost during an accounting period.

Direct costs: Those costs that can be traced directly to the sale of the goods or services of a business. As sales increase or decrease, so do direct costs. This is the test of whether an item is a direct or a fixed expense: If it *varies* with sales volume, it's a direct cost. If it must be paid regardless of sales, it's a fixed or overhead expense. In a manufacturing company, direct costs are tied to production rather than to sales: As production increases, so do direct costs. Direct costs include the cost of raw materials and of the labor required to turn them into finished products.

Direct labor: The cost of labor that can be directly traced to the sale of a company's products. Direct labor usually includes insurance and any fringe benefits associated with it. In a manufacturing company, direct labor is related to production rather than sales.

Direct materials: The cost of materials that can be traced directly to the finished product a company sells. Direct material costs usually include freight, a direct cost of getting the item to a store.

EBIT: Earnings before interest and taxes.

Earnings before interest and taxes: A business's net income before taxes have been paid and before any interest expense has been deducted.

Earnings power ratio: Calculated by dividing net sales by operating assets. It measures how effectively a company uses all its assets to produce profits.

Equity: The value of a business when all its liabilities are subtracted from its assets; also called *net worth*.

Equity ratios: Show the relationship between a business's debt and the owners' equity. The more a firm is owned by outside creditors, the more leveraged it is. The *owner's equity ratio* is calculated by dividing the owner's equity by the total assets of a company and reflects the percentage of the company owned by the shareholders.

Ending inventory: The amount of inventory on hand at the end of an accounting period.

Financial statement: A series of statements produced by a company or its accountant that show its condition at a particular point in time (balance sheet), how much income (or loss) it recorded over a period of time (income statement), and a statement that outlines what cash it received and what it did with it (flow of funds statement). Many financial statements also include detailed loan and depreciation worksheets, as well as other supporting information—anything that will help someone interpret the data.

Fixed asset: Something a business buys that it will not sell but use and that has an exact, or *fixed*, cost. It usually will be used for a number of years in the operation of a firm. Fixed assets are shown on a balance sheet *net* of accumulated depreciation.

Fixed cost: Something a company must pay whether or not it sells anything. Rent is an example of a fixed cost, as it must be paid whether or not the business records any sales. The test of a fixed cost is if it *varies* with sales volume. If it does, it's a variable (direct) cost. If it does not, it's a fixed cost.

Float: The funds represented in checks that haven't cleared the bank.

Flow of funds statement: A statement of a business's operations on a cash basis. Also called the *Statement of Change in Financial Position.*

Funds: Either cash or working capital. If funds are defined as cash, then all increases or decreases in cash will be shown on your Statement of Change in Financial Position. If they are defined as working capital, then every transaction that increases or decreases working capital will be shown on this statement.

Gross margin: Gross profit divided by revenues. A gross profit of $150,000 divided by revenues of $500,000 gives you a gross margin of 30%.

Gross profit: Cost of goods sold subtracted from revenue.

Income statement: A report that lists total sales, all related costs and expenses, and has as its bottom line the net income or loss during the period. Income statements always cover a specific period of time—one month, one year, etc.

Intangible assets: A nonphysical asset, such as goodwill, a covenant not to compete, patents, trademarks, or mailing lists. A business's investment in intangible assets can only be estimated; there's no accurate way to measure their value.

Interest: The charge made for the use of money borrowed (on a loan made with a bank; this would be listed as interest expense) or loaned customers (a finance charge that is added to past-due accounts receivable; this would be listed as interest income).

Inventory: Products on hand, ready for sale. In a manufacturing concern, inventory also includes raw materials and/or work in progress.

Inventory turnover rate: Measures the number of times a firm's inventory is sold over a particular period of time. It is calculated by dividing the cost of goods sold figure for the period under study by the average inventory during the same period. Dividing the number of days in a year by the resulting figure indicates how many days, on average, it took to sell the inventory.

Leverage: The use of other people's money in a company. The more others have invested in a business (either through a direct investment, loans, or a loan as an account payable) in relation to what the owner has invested, the more leveraged the company is.

Liabilities: A business's debts. Short-term, or current, liabilities are those due to be paid within the next year. Long-term liabilities are those that are due within a period longer than one year.

Liquidity: A measure of how well a business can satisfy its current obligations by testing to see how much of its assets are in the form of cash or can be quickly converted into cash.

Long-term debt: Obligations that do not require payment within one year.

Markdown: A decrease in price below its initial or expected selling price.

Markup: The amount of gross profit on an item.

Net income to net sales: Measures the percentage relationship between net sales and net income. It's calculated by dividing profits by net sales.

Net profit (also called net income): All cost of goods sold and expenses, including taxes, subtracted from all revenue.

Net sales: Sales revenue after any extraordinary items have been subtracted. If you sold some land during the last year, the sale might increase your profit line, but it really isn't part of the business's sales unless you're in real estate.

Net worth: Liabilities subtracted from assets; essentially, the *worth* or value of a business.

Note receivable: A receivable that has a formal note, or promise to pay in writing, associated with it.

Number of days of sales in accounts receivable: The number of days in the year divided by a business's accounts receivable turnover rate. This is also called the *average collection period,* and is designed to measure the average liquidity of a company's accounts receivable and to give some indication of their quality.

Operating cycle: The average time it takes for a business to *turn* its inventory (see *inventory turnover rate*) plus its average collection period (see *average collection period*). An operating cycle is the time it takes the money spent for inventory to return to the business in the form of cash—the whole transaction period.

Operating expenses: What it takes to run a business, even if it doesn't sell anything; also called *overhead.*

Overhead: The cost of running a business, whether or not it makes any sales.

Profit: Anything that's left when cost of goods sold and expenses are subtracted from revenue.

Purchases: Items bought, during a specific period, to be resold to customers.

Ratio: A measurement that compares one detail of financial data with another. These percentages let you compare companies of differing sizes (in terms of sales, total assets, total liabilities, and so on) with one another, as they are put on the same basis.

Receivables: see *accounts receivable.*

Receivables/sales ratio: Accounts receivable divided by sales.

Retained earnings: The portion of net profit that's retained in the business after any dividends or bonuses are paid; the amount of profit that stays in the business as part of its working capital.

Return on assets: Net income plus interest expense divided by the average investment in assets. This indicates a company's return, or earnings, on its assets.

Revenue: The flow into the business of assets (usually cash) that results from the delivery of products and/or service to a customer. Also called sales.

Safety margin: How much a business is recording as sales above its break-even point.

Selling expenses: The costs of storing inventory, promoting sales, selling products, and delivering and/or installing what has been sold.

Source of funds: A transaction that increases cash or working capital.

Statement of Change in Financial Position: A statement that details a company's cash operations during the period under study. The purpose of this statement is to explain what happened to all funds that came into the business and what those funds were used for. Also called the *Flow of Funds Statement*.

Tangible net worth: A company's book value after any intangible assets have been deducted (intangible assets include such things as goodwill, which are difficult to put a real value on).

Times interest earned ratio: A measurement of how much a company earned during a period of time compared with the interest it had to pay during that same period. The higher this ratio is, the safer any loan is, as the business is earning more in relation to the interest it must come up with. This figure is calculated by dividing income recorded before interest and taxes by total interest expense for the same period.

Total asset turnover: Divides net sales by average total assets and is a measurement of how effectively a company uses its assets. The more sales a company records from a given total asset base, the more effectively it is being run.

Trade payables: Same as accounts payable.

Useful life: The time period during which an asset is expected to be useful to the company.

Use of funds: A transaction that decreases cash or working capital.

Variable cost: An expense that varies with a business's sales.

Variance: Measures the difference between a company's financial expectations and the actual numbers.

Working capital: Current liabilities subtracted from current assets.

Magazine Bibliography

The articles listed below focus on the current literature of financial analysis for small businesses.

Bayer, Barry D. "How to Prepare a Trial-Balance Worksheet and Income Statement," *Computers in Accounting* (January/February 1985): 51–54.

Bennett, Thomas E. "Mixed Signals," *INC Magazine* (October 1987): 153.

Bernstein, Amy. "Manager's Eye View: Financial Modeling Software," *Business Computer Systems* (October 1985): 51–55.

Birch, David L. "The Booming Hidden Market," *INC Magazine* (October 1987): 15–16.

—— "The Rise and Fall of Everybody," *INC Magazine* (September 1987): 18–21.

Blank, Hannah L. "Bank Market Analysis on the PC," *PC Magazine* (September 4, 1984): 325–27.

Bock, Gordon, Geoff Lewis, and Marilyn A. Harris. "What's Wrong at IBM?" *Business Week* (March 12, 1986): 48–49.

Bodenstab, Charles J. "The Case for Accountability," *INC Magazine* (June 1988): 129–30.

—— "Flying Blind," *INC Magazine* (May 1988): 141–44.

Brody, Michael. "Back from the Brink," *Barrons* (January 2, 1984): 14, 30–31.

Brown, Paul B. "Bad Debt Can Be Good for Business," *INC Magazine* (March 1988): 119–22.

Campbell, Mary. "Make Financial Analysis Software Pay Off," *Business Computing* (September 1984): 68–70.

—— "How to Design Better Spreadsheet Forecasts," *Lotus* (May 1985): 72–77.

—— "Designing a Trend Analysis Report," *Lotus* (June 1985): 41–46.

—— "Minimizing Financial Costs," *Lotus* (September 1985): 52–54.

Crawford, Richard. "Streamlining Formulas," *Lotus* (February 1986): 70–74.

Edwards, Ken. "Mainframe Financial Modeling Comes to the Micro," *PC Magazine* (June 25, 1985): 165–72.

Fisher, Anne B. "Ford Is Back on the Track," *Fortune* (December 23, 1985): 18–22.

Forrest, N. B. "Heavy-Duty PC Forecasting," *PC Magazine* (July 9, 1985): 231–33.

—— "Forecasting Tools for the Business Manger," *PC Magazine* (June 25, 1986): 257–59.

Freid, Louis. "Tools of the Manager's Trade: Expert Systems Enter the Corporate Domain," *Management Technology* (January 1985): 58–63.

Getzler, Abraham E. "How to Spot Hidden Threats to Your Business," *Nation's Business* (January 1983): 69–70.

Glau, Gregory R. "Cash Flow Woes," *inCider* (January 1984): 152–54.

—— "A Lotus Worksheet for Cash Planning," *Computers in Accounting* (November/December 1985): 50–54.

—— "1-2-3 Budget Tune-Up" *PC World* (January 1987): 272–78.

Gordon, John B. "Adjusting Data for Seasonal Patterns," *Lotus* (March 1986): 62–65.

Green, James H. "Using Life-Cycle Analysis," *Lotus* (August 1985): 51–54.

Greene, Richard. "The Missing Number," *Forbes* (June 18, 1984): 123.

Grubb, Robert. "Expert Describes Warning Signs of Business Failure," *Colorado Business Review* (May 1985): 41–42.

Gumbert, David E. "Playing it Straight," *INC Magazine* (April 1988): 140–41.

Hawkens, Paul. "Mastering the Numbers," *INC Magazine* (October 1987): 19–20.

Hohenstein, C. Louis. "A Template for Preparing a Cash-Flow Forecast," *Computers in Accounting* (September/October 1984): 33–39.

Hollman, Elli. "A Plan for the Future," *Personal Computing* (October 1983): 74–79.

Horwitt, Elisabeth. "Keeping Company Resources on Course," *Business Computer Systems* (August 1983): 52–60.

Hughes, G. David. "To Lease or to Buy?" *Business Computer Systems* (February 1984): 43–46.

—— "Pricing for Profit," *Business Computer Systems* (April 1984): 31–33.

—— "The Litmus Test for Pricing Strategies," *Business Computer Systems* (December 1983): 41–42.

—— "How to Analyze Sales Performance," *Business Computer Systems* (January 1984): 17–20.

—— "When Inventory Means Sales," *Business Computer Systems* (July 1984): 33–34, 39.

Hunt, Donald. "Formulas for Profit," *PC World* (December 1984): 286–94.

Hutchins, Dexter. "And Now, the Home-Brewed Forecast," *Fortune* (January 20, 1986): 53–54.

INC Magazine. "Waging War on Business Failure" (August 1983): 109.

Jones, Edward. "Risk Analysis with 1-2-3," *Lotus* (July 1985): 65–67.

Kaplan, Robert (interview), *INC Magazine* (April 1988): 54–67.

Kelleher, Joanne. "Tackling Information Management," *Business Computer Systems* (October 1985): 65–68.

—— "Human Factors," *Business Computer Systems* (August 1985): 65–66, 70–71.

—— "New Help for Personnel," *Business Computer Systems* (February 1984): 90–98.

Kennedy, Marilyn Moats. "10 Ways to Tell if your Company's Going Under," *Working Woman* (September 1985): 132–33.

Kyd, Charles W. "Using the Power of Break-Even Analysis," *Lotus* (June 1985): 29–38.

—— "Scheduling Your Cash Requirements," *Lotus* (August 1985): 43–46.

—— "Forecasting Bankruptcy with Z Scores," *Lotus* (September 1985): 43–47.

—— "Determining Sustainable Growth," *Lotus* (February 1986): 45–52.

—— "Excuses, Excuses," *INC Magazine* (August 1987): 87–88.

—— "Getting the Cash out of Cash Flow," *INC Magazine* (July 1987): 87–88.

Labick, Kenneth. "Is Business Taking on Too Much Debt?" *Fortune* (July 22, 1985): 82–85.

Levin, Paul. "Cost Accounting for Construction Jobs," *PC Magazine* (September 18, 1984): 327–29.

Mace, Scott. "Business Simulations Graduate into the Real World," *Info-World* (February 17, 1986): 37–38.

Mamis, Robert A. "Lender of Last Resort," *INC Magazine* (May 1987): 149.

—— "Can this Company Be Saved?" *INC Magazine* (October 1987): 92–100.

McComas, Maggie. "Riches to Rags at Delta Drilling," *Fortune* (September 16, 1985): 57–62.

McGrath, Frank. "Simplifying Your Credit Decisions," *Lotus* (February 1986): 57–61.

Meadows, Laura Lou. "Keeping the Wolves at Bay," *PC Magazine* (May 15, 1985): 269–74.

Miles, J. B. "Toward a Model Modeler," *Computer Decisions* (July 15, 1985): 92–96, 96D, 122.

Miller, James C. "Use 1-2-3 to Consolidate Data from Several Users," *Computers in Accounting* (March/April 1986): 48–59.

Monk, Thomas J. and Kenneth M. Landis. "Saying Goodbye to Budget Blues," *Business Computer Systems* (July 1983): 23–24.

Nelson, Stephen L. "The Budget," *Lotus* (May 1988): 66–72.

––––––– "Cash Flow," *Lotus* (June 1988): 77–81.

Pittel, Leslie. "Cherchez la Cash," *Forbes* (June 3, 1985): 234–36.

Rubin, Charles. "Getting a Firm Grasp of Business Fundamentals," *Personal Computing* (November 1983): 33–37.

––––––– "Beating the Budget Crunch," *Personal Computing* (November 1983): 88–94, 228.

––––––– "Forecasting via Spreadsheet," *Personal Computing* (September 1984): 177–91.

––––––– "Visual Decision Support," *Personal Computing* (February 1985): 101–09.

Rutledge, John. "Fortune Telling: Keep Your Eye on the Trends, Not the Details," *INC Magazine* (January 1985): 12–13.

St. Gvar, Jinny. "Where's the Cash?" *Forbes* (April 4, 1985): 120.

Saporito, Bill. "Scott Isn't Lumbering Anymore," *Fortune* (September 30, 1985): 48–55.

Sirota, Walter. "A New Focus on Data Management," *PC World* (February 1985): 216–25.

Stahr, Lisa B. "The Corporate Computer," *PC World* 1.3 (September 1983): 296–301.

––––––– "Working with Statistical Analysis," *Personal Computing* (October 1984): 97–107.

Suters, Everett T. "Show and Tell," *INC Magazine* (April 1987): 111–12.

Walden, Jeffrey. "The Template Question," *Business Computer Systems* (December 1984): 62–64.

Williams, Andrew T. "Of Spreadsheets and Models," *PC World* (November 1984): 66–70.

Woodwell, Don. "PCs in Forecasting," *PC Magazine* (December 25, 1984): 297–300.

Young, Jeffrey. "Computer Graphics: Toys or Tools?" *Personal Computing* (March 1985): 53–59.

––––––– "Taking the Pain out of Planning," *PC Magazine* (May 1, 1984): 164–68.

Zarley, Craig. "Managing Cash Flow for the Profit of It," *Personal Computing* (November 1983): 127–35, 235.

Book Bibliography

Alves, Jeffrey R., Dennis P. Curtin, and Anne K. Briggs. *Planning and Budgeting for Higher Profits* (New York: Van Nostrand Reinhold, 1983), 170 pp., $15.50.

Anderson, Anker V. *Graphing Financial Information: How Accountants Can Use Graphs to Communicate* (New York: The National Association of Accountants, 1983), 51 pp., $6.95.

Backer, Morton and Martin L. Gosman. *Financial Reporting and Business Liquidity* (Montvale, NJ: National Association of Accountants), 305 pp., $24.95.

Bernstein, Leopold. *The Analysis of Financial Statements*, rev. ed. (Homewood, IL: Dow Jones-Irwin, 1978), 381 pp., $25.

Camillus, John C. *Budgeting for Profit: How to Exploit the Potential of Your Business* (Radnor, PA: Chilton Book Company, 1984), 192 pp., $19.95.

Cohen, Neil and Lois Graff. *Financial Analysis with Lotus 1-2-3* (Bowie, MD: Brady Communications Company, 1984), 317 pp., $15.50.

Curtain, Dennis P., Jeffrey R. Alves, and Anne K. Briggs. *Controlling Financial Performance for Higher Profits* (New York: Van Nostrand Reinhold, 1983), 170 pp., $15.50.

Dixon, Robert L. *The Executive's Accounting Primer* (New York: McGraw-Hill, 1971), 328 pp.

Edwards, James Don et al. *How Accounting Works—A Guide for the Perplexed* (Homewood, Illinois: Dow Jones-Irwin, 1983), 374 pp., $19.95.

Glau, Gregory R. *Controlling Your Cash Flow with 1-2-3- or Symphony* (Homewood, IL: Dow Jones-Irwin, 1986), 198 pp., $19.95.

—— *Business Graphics for the IBM PC/XT/AT* (Homewood, IL: Dow Jones-Irwin, 1986), 323 pp., $19.95.

Greenfield, W. M. and Dennis P. Curtin. *Cash Flow Management with Lotus 1-2-3* (Englewood Cliffs, NJ: Prentice-Hall/Curtain & London, 1985), 152 pp., $21.95. (There is also an edition covering Symphony.)

Haller, Terry. *Secrets of the Master Business Strategists* (Englewood Cliffs, NJ: Prentice-Hall, 1983), 218 pp., $10.95.

Harvard Business Review on Management (New York: Harper & Row, 1975), 751 pp.

Jarrett, Irwin M. *Computer Graphics & Reporting Financial Data* (New York: Ronald Press, 1983), 360 pp., $49.95. Distributed by John Wiley & Sons.

Lowry, Albert. *How to Become Financially Successful by Owning Your Own Business* (New York: Simon and Schuster, 1981), 407 pp., $14.95.

Miller, Donald E. *The Meaningful Interpretation of Financial Statements* (New York: American Management Associations, 1979), 232 pp., $6.95.

Osteryoung, Jerome S. and Daniel E. McCarty. *Analytical Techniques for Financial Management* (New York: John Wiley & Sons, 1985), 282 pp., $14.95.

Owens, Robert R., Daniel R. Garner, and Dennis S. Bunder. *The Arthur Young Guide to Financing for Growth* (New York: John Wiley & Sons, 1986), 298 pp., $29.95.

Peters, Thomas J. and Robert H. Waterman, Jr. *In Search of Excellence* (New York: Harper & Row, 1982).

Toncré, Emery. *Maximizing Cash Flow.* (New York: John Wiley & Sons, 1986), 210 pp., $19.95.

Tracy, John. *How to Read a Financial Report* (New York: John Wiley & Sons, 1980), 156 pp.

Uris, Auren. *The Executive Deskbook*, 2nd ed. (New York: Van Nostrand Reinhold, 1976), 330 pp., $10.25.

Winston, Stephanie. *The Organized Executive* (New York: W. W. Norton & Co., 1983), 345 pp.

Wortman, Leon A. *Successful Small Business Management* (New York: American Management Associations, 1978), 262 pp., $8.95.

Index